FOUNDATION TO SUSTAINABLE SUCCESS

A Conscious Guide to Mastering the Mortgage Business

KELLY RESENDEZ

This publication is designed to provide accurate and authoritative information in regard to the subject matter covered. It is sold with the understanding that neither the author nor the publisher is engaged in rendering accounting, legal, investment, or other professional service through the writing of this book. There is no guarantee, expressed or implied, that by following the information in this book you will earn money or improve current profits.

Library of Congress Control Number: 2017912067

ISBN: 978-0-9990461-0-4

First Printing: August, 2017

Published by: 102nd Place, LLC
Scottsdale, AZ

Printed in the United States of America

To my mom, Marlene Goodman.

I know you are dancing in heaven knowing you helped me grow into the woman I am today.

TABLE OF CONTENTS

———

INTRODUCTION

"Success is never a destination—it's a journey."
— Satenig St. Marie —

Benjamin Franklin once wrote, ". . . in this world nothing can be said to be certain, except death and taxes." If you work in the mortgage industry you can add one more caveat to that. The mortgage market will be ever-changing and always challenging.

Interest rates fall, inventory is great, demand is high, business is good; interest rates rise, inventory is tight, demand diminishes, business is bad—at least that's what many of us have come to believe. It's a convenient excuse for our lack of production and the consequent reduction in our earnings. It's true we can't control interest rate fluctuations or how many homes are listed for sale. But we can control our own business strategies and practices. It is possible to create a sustainable business, even in times of rising interest rates or low inventory.

Customers have many options when shopping for mortgage products and a mortgage provider. To build a sustainable business, you must be ahead of the curve. You need to focus on increasing the quantity and quality of the opportunities you have and the rate at which you convert them. You must also be open to reinventing yourself or your business often to adapt to the changing market.

The purpose of building a sustainable, systematic business is so you can concentrate your efforts on the activities that have the highest return—mainly building relationships and reacting creatively to changes in the market. Burn-out and lack of follow-through are high in this industry. You have to have the discipline and determination to push through the layers of chaos and industry ups and downs to continue to be successful regardless of market conditions.

So if that's all we have to do—put in place strategies and systems to be more successful and happier—then why don't we just do it? There are tons of books and loads of information and step-by-step guides available in book stores and on the internet. You've probably tried a few of them. Maybe some of them even worked for a while. But none of them lasted. Why?

The answer lies within each of us—not in some book, or seminar, or weekly sales meeting. It's our mental attitudes, our emotional triggers, and our self-sabotaging behaviors that are holding us back. Don't get me wrong, we need systems and strategies. But we also need to be open to examining our own imperfections, shame, guilt, or whatever it is that is sabotaging our ability to create the business and personal life we truly desire. This also includes diminishing the power our egos have over us and choosing to put our hearts in charge.

Foundation to Sustainable Success will guide you to do just that. Yes I'll tell you about goal setting, give you processes you need to do regularly, and give you tips on how to gather and retain referral partners among other things. But first, we must start with your mindset and core beliefs, those things that are the current foundation for who you are. We'll need to discover what to keep, what to change, and what to purge. We'll need to build a new foundation. Only then will we be able to layer on the strategies and systems to create sustainable success.

First we'll talk about why you want to have a sustainable business and what forces are at work that help or hinder that process.

Then we'll take a deeper dive into what constitutes real success. It's not the same for everyone. You may be surprised to find out how much our brains play a role in this.

Once we understand the concepts of sustainability and success we're ready to jump into building our foundation. Level 1 brings us to the meat of the change that we must undergo in order to create a sustainable business. It is all about who we are "being" in our business. We'll explore areas such as emotional intelligence, stress, triggers, and sabotage management. This is Level 1 of our foundation. These are the core behaviors that we need to have under control before any "system" will work.

Level 2 delves into the creation of our second layer. Here is where we'll start to talk about the strategies that you need to have in place. What's your vision? What are your goals? Who is your ideal client? Who is your ideal referral partner? What's your marketing plan? Where Level 1 concentrates on your emotional being, Level 2 concentrates on your mental being—the planning portion of your sustainable system.

The final layer, Level 3, in our foundation is execution. Here you'll learn the specific actions you must take. I know many of you will be tempted to jump right to this chapter. I get it—it's easier to just "do it!" right? If you do—you'll have wasted your time and your money on this book. Taking action won't get you where you want to be if you are not emotionally and mentally prepared.

I've been in the mortgage industry for more than 20 years. I know what it feels like when the highs are high, and the lows are low. But I've learned it doesn't have to be that way. It is possible, with some hard work and self-examination to break out of the habits and patterns that sabotage you.

I am hoping this book starts a movement that raises awareness and professionalism in our industry. It saddens me to see so many ego-driven and money-hungry mortgage people define our industry. The entitlement has to end and we need to start treating people better and elevate our businesses. You can be wildly prosperous and egoless at the same time but it will take work. We have a responsibility to develop ourselves and our value so that it never becomes commoditized. I understand that most companies don't promote this idea so I hope you will put in the energy and time for yourself and your business.

To your sustainable success!

Kelly Resendez

SUSTAINABILITY

———

*"The world is round and the place which may
seem like the end may also be the beginning."*
— Ivy Baker Priest —

What if you woke up each morning free from worry about the status of your business? What if you knew with confidence that all the pieces were in place for your continued success? What if you could create a business you love and find joy doing it?

If you think that sounds too good to be true, think again. Developing a sustainable business and income stream is not only possible but doable, without a lot of stress and frustration. I've done it, and so have the loan officers who've taken and applied the ideas I'll share with you in this book.

So what do I mean by sustainability? *The New Oxford American Dictionary* defines it as: the ability to be maintained at a certain rate or level; continuing for an extended period or without interruption.

When I talk about sustainability in the mortgage business, I'm talking about having a consistent, reliant stream of new loans and subsequent income regardless of what is happening around you.

There are several factors that affect your ability to attain sustainability. The most important of which is you. We'll delve into that in great detail in later chapters. For now, let's start with some of the outside factors.

Market Changes

If you read the Introduction, you already know that one of the things in the mortgage business that we can count on is market changes. Inventory, the overall economy, and consumer confidence drive the demand for new housing. In addition, the availability of loan programs and products sets the tempo for the types of mortgages we can offer. And then of course, there is the ever present interest rate effect.

How can you possibly create a sustainable business model with all of these variables at play? It's all about focusing on the right things.

Let's take the overall mortgage market for example. It's divided into purchases and refinances. When interest rates go down, generally refinances go up. When interest rates go up, refinances drop. But that's not true with the purchase market. If someone needs, or wants, to buy a house they are going to buy a house regardless of what interest rates are doing. The purchase market is more "sustainable" than the refi market.

Putting your focus on developing a sustainable flow of purchase referrals that are not tied to interest rates is the most effective strategy.

However, purchase behavior among consumers is also changing. Millennials are more educated, more online savvy and more apt to take an eCommerce approach to finding a loan originator. They may prefer online applications and text messages to the reams of paper and phone calls that their parents or grandparents preferred.

To generate sustainability, you must be creative and innovative in how you reach and communicate with these different buyers. To some extent, this will be dependent on who you define as your ideal client; because again you'll want to focus on activities that will bring those clients to you. We'll talk about that in the second level of building our foundation.

Run Your Business like a Business

Many people enter the mortgage origination business because they like the freedom. They want the ability to earn at a higher level and to some extent, be their own boss.

What they don't seem to fully grasp however, is that when they become a lender they also become a business owner. This key fact is often lost. Many people don't know what to do with the freedom that working 100% on commission allows. Perhaps they've come from a corporate job, or maybe they've just graduated from college. They are used to having others tell them what to do. They come into the business with an employee mentality.

If you want to create sustainability, then you must think and act like a business owner. You need a business model that defines goals and activities. You need to have the metrics in place to measure the efficiency of what you are doing. You need to understand the return on investment of your time and resources.

For example, most people in this industry don't know where their referrals come from. Is that marketing plan you spent hundreds on bringing you referrals? Or is working your database consistently the main generator? You need to be able to answer these questions if you hope to build a sustainable business. You need a predictable model.

Create a Predictable Model

Predictability comes in measuring activities and efficiency rates for getting referrals—the lifeblood of this business. What happens far too often is that lenders get lazy when times are good. They become reactive order takers; too busy they think to maintain the activities that will keep business coming to them when things slow down.

And when business does slow down, they quickly fall into a scarcity mindset. Scarcity leads to excuses, to blaming something or someone other than ourselves for the results we are achieving. A scarcity mindset is the enemy of sustainability.

It takes discipline to keep the scarcity mindset at bay. It takes having a plan that you work the same way regardless of how busy you are. It takes doing activities that you know will generate business consistently no matter what.

If you stop working your plan, your plan will stop working. It's really that simple. This business is all risk, all the time. Working by referral does not mean you accept referrals when someone sends them to you. It means developing referral partners and referral pipelines that will consistently send business your way.

You must be actively focused on earning partner referrals from the very beginning. If you build a predictable referral model, and you keep the discipline to work it even when you are busy, you can create sustainability for the rest of your career.

Take Motivation out of the Equation

I cringe every time I hear a loan originator say, "Doing that just doesn't motivate me." Motivation is "nice to have." It's nice to get an extra bonus when you meet a certain number. It's nice to rub elbows with the rest of the top producers on an all-expense paid Caribbean cruise. But seriously, if you truly believe that outside "motivators" are what keep these producers at the top, you are sadly mistaken.

The nuts and bolts of your foundation, the activities that you must do every day to build a sustainable business, are not motivating. That's the truth. The majority of people don't wake up in the morning excited to do the things they need to do to work their foundation. Those are boring tasks; not sexy, or exciting. But performing them anchors you into certainty. Performing them enables you to deal more easily with this industry's inherent risk.

Those top producers? They're at the top because they understand how important it is to do the mundane tasks: cold calling agents, booking appointments, entering information into their database. They do those things even when they don't feel like doing them.

Building sustainability is about repetitiveness. It's about doing the same things every day that you know will make you successful.

But nobody said you have to do it alone. If you really can't stand to make one more cold call or schedule one more meeting, then find someone who can support your foundation and start building an internal team or outsource more of the things you don't want to do.

DEFINING SUCCESS

—

"Success is liking yourself, liking what you do,
and liking how you do it."
— Maya Angelou —

I've said time and again that building a sustainable foundation is what you need to do in order to be a success in this business. But what is success?

Tangible Result or Feeling?

Most people define success through their accumulated life experiences, by comparing themselves to others (loan officers or top producers), or by listening to friends and family recount their versions of success. If we define our success by what other people think or feel, we are in essence setting ourselves up for failure.

The actual components of success for each of us may be as different as our fingerprints. But in my experience there are basically two types of individuals when it comes to defining success: those who define it by tangible results and those who define it as a feeling.

If you're a person who defines success by tangible results then you may say things like: "I'll be successful when my paycheck is x amount, or I'll be successful when I close x number of deals every month, or I'll be successful when I make top producer."

Conversely, a person who defines success by a feeling might say things like: "I'll be successful when I no longer have to worry about money, or I'll be successful when others are envious of me, or I'll be successful when I'm not anxious about when I'll get my next referral."

The thing tangible results and feelings have in common when defining success is that they are usually set sometime in the future. There's no appreciation for the successes of here and now. I've known consistent top producers who never feel successful even though the numbers and their peers say they are. Why is this? Why are we reluctant to define success in the moment? It all has to do with our brains.

Self-Definition

Yes, our brains—wonderfully functioning machines that they are—could actually be working against us when it comes to being successful and recognizing that we are. Up until about 2007, most neuroscientists and doctors believed that our brain was "hard-wired." That once we reached adulthood we were stuck with what we had. But then scientists from Harvard ran some studies that proved the brain is more "soft-wired." It can evolve and change as the information and sensory data we feed to it changes.

What happens with many of us is that once we've achieved "success" our brain immediately kicks in and says—nope, not good enough, you have to do better, you can do better, Larry or Shirley did better, etc., etc. It automatically moves success further and further out because of past learned behavior.

Maybe we're always comparing ourselves to others. Maybe our family and friends do the comparing for us. Maybe we're trying to live up to others' expectations. Maybe we've been made to feel "not good enough" on more than one occasion. By allowing others to define success on our behalf, we've taught our brains not to celebrate success in the here and now but always be reaching for something more.

The great thing about the Harvard study and others like it is that it proved the brain can't distinguish between a real and an imagined event. That's why our dreams can often feel real. So by learning how to control our thoughts we can deliberately rewire our brains to make ourselves more successful and fulfilled. Simply thinking and seeing ourselves as successful is the first step to eventually making success a reality.

I'm going to talk a lot more about this in Level 1 of building your foundation. But here are a few things you can do right away to start to rewire your brain for success:

1. Resist the urge to use self-defeating language. For example, if something goes wrong, like you miss an important meeting, don't call yourself stupid or an idiot. Say something positive like, "I've learned that I need a better system for scheduling." Don't use words like "I can't," say instead "When I am able . . . ."

2. Control your environment. Surround yourself with people who are positive and supporting, not negative or demeaning. Keep in mind too, that since our brain can't distinguish between what's real and what isn't, just listening to 30 minutes of sensationalized news or 30 minutes of gossip or complaining, makes it feel like we've experienced it first-hand.

3. Get used to using superlatives, even if you think you might sound a bit corny. For example, don't say "I'm fine." Instead say, "I'm awesome, or I'm absolutely amazing!"

4. Don't say I am busy or overwhelmed. It is hard to feel successful at the same time you are complaining. Your brain may shut you down if you continuously do this. Telling people you are too busy also sends the message you can't handle more business.

If you take control of your thoughts in this way, if you are conscious and consistent in thinking positively and pro-actively, then you will begin to truly experience success.

The quicker you can start to celebrate the small stuff, the faster your brain will rewire itself toward success as a natural part of your life. You need to create a feeling of owning your week. It isn't just about the business results but what did you do? Did you do what you set out to do? Yes? Then celebrate that success. Were you accountable to yourself, did you have an ambitious week and worked hard? Yes? Then celebrate that success. The simple cure to success and happiness is to make yourself do the things you don't want to do when you are actually supposed to do them. Then celebrate your awesome discipline!

This is an ego-driven occupation and it's hard not to do comparisons. But comparisons often lead to excuses which are self-defeating talk. It doesn't matter what the other guy did—it matters what you did and that you were true to yourself. The rest will come as you reset your brain for success. Remember, success is not a destination—it's a journey. You must be ready for it to be a marathon and not a sprint. If you get caught up in discontentment because other people are succeeding faster, you will derail your own potential.

BUILDING THE FOUNDATION

"... we have a tendency to obscure the forest of simple joys with the trees of problems."
— Christiane Collange —

Quite simply put, the foundation is what everything rests on. In construction the foundation is built of poured concrete footers. They are one of the most critical aspects of the building because they spread the weight of the structure across a wider footprint.

Foundations may be shallow—going only a few inches down into the weak top soil, or they may be deep—solidly placed further down into the much stronger sub-soil layer. This analogy works particularly well when talking about building a foundation for sustainable success.

I spoke earlier about you being the key element in building this foundation. Think of yourself as the "footer." Are you shallow or are you deep? In other words, do you know what makes you tick? Are you in tune with your emotions and those of others around you? Are you emotionally intelligent and do you know how to apply this intelligence to build a sustainable business?

Emotional intelligence is a term that first came into wide use sometime around 1995. People who are emotionally intelligent can manage their emotions, even the negative ones, and still achieve their intended goals. Emotional intelligence guides their thinking and their behavior and allows them to adapt quickly to changing environments.

There are two main competencies that make up emotional intelligence: personal and social. The most important in laying down the footers of your foundation is personal competency. That is what we will be discussing in Levels 1 and 2. I'll talk about social competency, which deals with social awareness and relationship management, in Level 3.

Self-awareness: your ability to recognize your emotions and stay aware of them as they happen; and self-management: the ability to use that awareness to stay flexible and positively direct your behavior, are the two major components of personal competency.

Everyone can develop emotional intelligence and use it to their advantage. Remember our brains are not "hard-wired." The pathway for emotional intelligence starts at the spinal cord. All of your experiences and senses enter here and have to travel to the front of your brain in order for you to think rationally about them. But before they get there they must pass through the limbic system. This is where emotions are generated. That means we always have an emotional reaction to every experience before we have a rational one.

Personality also plays a role in our emotional intelligence. According to Dr. Travis Bradberry, "Personality consists of a stable set of preferences and tendencies through which we approach the world." I'm going to talk about preferences in detail later on. What's important to note here is what type of personality you believe you have: extrovert, introvert, or a combination of the two, ambivert.

Personality traits, like your belief systems, develop from an early age. But while it is possible to change your belief systems it is highly unlikely that you will change your personality type. This is mainly due to the fact that personality relies on the amount of dopamine that occurs naturally in your system. If you have a large amount of dopamine then you need less outside stimulation and you will most likely be an introvert. Less amounts of dopamine require more outside stimulation so you would tend to be an extrovert. Those with average levels, the majority of us, are ambiverts.

Becoming aware of your type is important because it allows you to understand your tendencies and play to your strengths. Contrary to popular opinion, extroverts do not make the best salespeople. Ambiverts do. The reason is their personality doesn't lean too much one way or the other. They can be much more flexible and may have an easier time adjusting to different situations.

Becoming self-aware and then retraining our brains to respond differently based on emotional intelligence enables us to develop consistent behaviors that will aid us in building a sustainable business. Let's take a look at the areas of emotional intelligence we need to retrain so you can show up as your best and highest self.

LEVEL 1
WHO YOU ARE BEING

———

"We don't see things as they are,
we see them as we are."
— Anaïs Nin —

Mindset and Core Beliefs

"Progress is impossible without change
and those who cannot change
their mind cannot change anything."
— George Bernard Shaw —

If we truly want to be more successful in our business and personal lives, and sustain that success year after year, we must constantly and consistently be aware of our mindset. The 2010 edition of the *New Oxford American Dictionary* describes mindset as: the established set of attitudes held by someone. I also like to define it as the core beliefs an individual has about life and business. These core beliefs make up the basis for your current level of emotional intelligence.

Core beliefs begin in childhood and develop over time. They are the essence of how we see ourselves, other people, the world, and the future. Often influenced by the values of our families and communities they can be rigid and inflexible. We maintain them by focusing on only those things that support our beliefs and dismissing or ignoring evidence that contradicts them.

For example, when I ask people if they think of themselves as optimists or pessimists, 90% of the time they will tell me they are optimists. If I ask their spouse or their kids the same question they'll say, "Are you kidding? You complain and worry about stuff all the time! Nothing seems to make you happy; definitely a pessimist."

This is exactly the crux of the problem. Many of us don't even know what our mindset is. We've lived with our beliefs for so long that we're no longer consciously aware of them. So the big question is: can you shift your beliefs? The good news is that we can. We can challenge our thinking and replace it with more balanced thoughts—thoughts that serve our greater good.

Perhaps one of the easiest ways to begin to uncover those core beliefs that no longer serve you is to pay attention to the words that come out of your mouth or the unspoken thoughts you are having. Are you always complaining? Do you often think, why me or what is wrong with me? Is your first thought when something doesn't go according to plan—Oh no, I'm screwed? The more you pay attention to the negative things you say or think, the more you can ask yourself, why am I feeling that way? Is it really because you don't believe you deserve to have things go well? Were your parents always quick to blame someone else for their problems and are you simply modeling what you saw growing up?

Emotions and the feelings behind those emotions are the keys to discovering what you truly believe. When you understand what you believe and why you believe it, you have the ability to change that belief for the better. Take the example of the parents who were always quick to blame someone else. They may have done this because they subconsciously felt guilty for not being prepared. Or maybe they felt shame about not having enough knowledge to avoid the situation. They may have taught you to avoid accepting responsibility for your part. When you look at yourself, do these same values apply? If you are quick to blame others and have a hard time seeing your faults, this is an area you will want to work on.

Mindset is a key component in determining success. Identifying and changing the core beliefs in our minds can eliminate the uncomfortable emotions and sabotaging behaviors that we've used as compensating strategies in our lives up until now. We can cultivate the right mindset that will not only aid us but also enable us to help many of the people who come in and out of our lives.

I wish changing your mindset was as easy as Rhonda Byrne in *The Secret* makes it sound. But the law of attraction isn't just about thinking it and it will come. If that were the case we'd all have exactly what we want when we want it and we'd all be happy. We still need to take action. We must show up differently and be committed and intentional every day about staying in our new mindset. We cannot allow our thoughts and emotions to control us any longer.

While you sleep, your brain takes all the thoughts you had during the day and draws them deeper into your life. If you think negatively, that life is hard then hard is what you will attract. The thoughts you have when you go to bed and the thoughts you have when you first wake up are the two most important decisions you can make. It isn't always easy work, but the rewards are significant.

A successful mindset is made up of many attributes and beliefs. Here are a few that can make a significant impact to your success.

1. **Growth minded**—nothing is fixed, nothing is hard-wired. As far as your business is concerned you can do better, you can become stronger, and you can manage your thoughts and emotions so that they serve you instead of you serving them.

You can grow through any problem or roadblock and know when it is time to avoid certain things or set new boundaries.

2. **Purpose driven**—you know your "why?" Why, out of all the occupations you could have chosen, did you decide to be a loan originator? If your why is because you want to make a lot of money then you won't sustain success. Money motivation is not long-lasting. The why that sustains success is the why that explains your purpose in wanting to provide loans. How are you helping and who are you helping? How will your success provide for your family and impact other people's lives? This is your leverage in striving to achieve your goals.

3. **Value driven**—you know what your values are and they are unshakable. For example, if integrity is one of your values and someone asks you to do something wrong, you won't do it no matter what. Your plan is made in alignment with your values to ensure you have your priorities straight and will feel good about what you are doing.

4. **Business minded**—I've talked about this before and I'll discuss it in detail later on but you must have goals, a business plan, and the discipline to work the plan. It constantly amazes me that 95% of loan officers don't have a business plan. Without a plan you will miss out on a lot of opportunity and have no idea how to replicate or increase your

success. When we don't have a plan we might pour money and energy into marketing ideas or referral sources that don't yield enough opportunity to warrant them.

You need to have a budget and understand your return on investment (ROI). I wish I had a dollar for every time I've heard someone tell me that lead generation doesn't work. I'd be a wealthy woman. Tell the owners of Zillow that. The problem is you aren't working it the right way because you don't know your ROI.

You have to be accountable. You should wake up every morning and do what you say you're going to do whether you feel like it or not. Remember discipline not motivation is what makes for a sustainable business.

5. **Priorities are straight**—you know what is most important. You know if you keep your priorities in line then you will be happy in your work. If you're not happy your clients can tell. No one wants to work with someone who is so out of balance that they're too busy to pay attention to relationship needs. When you look at your calendar and check-book is it reflective of your real priorities? Are you spending time and money on the things that are most important to you?

6. **Focus is on abundance not scarcity**—I already spoke about how the freedom in this industry can

quickly lead to a mindset of scarcity. When we're not doing what we're supposed to, and business starts to taper off, we begin to worry that there's not enough pie to go around.

A person with an abundant mindset says the pie is just going to keep getting bigger for me. I'm always going to have everything I need. If I lose a client, I'm going to get two more. If you're not in a state of abundance you are most likely attracting things that may make you worry and suffer.

General Beliefs

General beliefs are a part of your mindset that you might need to be reminded of often. You may already believe them or they may be new to you. Adopting them as part of who you are will help you stay disciplined when life gets hard or your problems trigger you. Reviewing them often and ensuring they are included in your goals and business plan will set you up for sustainable success. Here are the proven beliefs of top performing loan officers:

1. Opportunity and Lead Creation is the number one priority. This is why you make commission. You are paid to hunt for new business. You must balance both managing the business you already have and creating new business. As your pipeline grows you cannot forget to spend at least 50% of your time on this.

2. I MUST adapt to market changes quickly. I will not get caught up in feeling sorry for myself or waiting for things to return to how they were. I will seek new opportunities immediately or increase my activity levels to adjust to wherever the market is.

3. I MUST plan for roadblocks and problems. I accept they are unavoidable. In order to be a top performer I cannot allow them to cause a disruption in my business or state. I know my value comes from remaining disciplined despite anything that goes wrong. I will always use problems or challenges to improve my business. I will accept that any road-block is there for me to push through or move in a different direction.

4. I believe everyone does the best they can. Rather than blaming or shaming others I will see any disappointment as an opportunity to be more accepting of our humanness. I believe everyone intends to help me and any mistake or challenge is there to help my business improve or me to anticipate better.

5. I am detached from outcomes. I know expecting of others only leads to disappointment. I will always do the best I can and be clear about what is needed from others. I will hold people accountable yet not let it affect me emotionally if they don't perform. I trust everything always works out the way it should.

6. I have strong boundaries and say no easily. I recognize there is a human capacity to what I can handle. I know I need downtime and plan it accordingly. I will not fight other people's battles and will be armed against distractions. I will remain focused on my vision, goals, plan, and priorities as I schedule my time.

7. I know I cannot please everyone or make everyone happy. I recognize that setting boundaries and remaining detached will be uncomfortable for some referral partners or clients but I will stay committed to it. I will do my best all the time and remain truthful even if it makes others unhappy.

8. I welcome and learn from criticism. I welcome all feedback as a way to become more emotionally intelligent or better at my job. I will not allow my ego to deflect or project any discomfort from it.

9. I will not compare myself to others or envy what others receive or have. I will stick to my own vision, goals, plan, and priorities regardless of what others are doing. I recognize that any comparison or envy is produced by my ego and does not serve me.

10. I recognize I need to learn how to think differently. I will be more disciplined about responding and not reacting. I believe I am not my thoughts or emotions and have the power to choose a new mindset.

11. I will allow faith to guide me over fear. I know my ego is producing fear only to protect me but I will

override this daily with a strong belief I must leave my comfort zone to achieve sustainable success. I believe every failure or instance that I am rejected will guide me to more opportunity.

12. I must manage my reactions to the predictable triggers that exist in this industry. I will not allow them to derail my energy or focus.

You may identify other core beliefs that have helped you succeed in the past that can be added to this list. I have found getting super clear about what I believe helps me stay centered when things get chaotic and I am seduced into negativity by others around me.

Power of I AM Statements

One thing that works for me in maintaining a positive and successful mindset is to focus on a series of "I AM" statements each morning. These are statements that describe who I need to be in order to run a sustainable business and cultivate the energy I need. For example: I am patient, I am clear, I am smart, I am courageous, I am grateful, I am helpful, I am prospering, I am disciplined, I am . . . .

I encourage you to make your own list of I AM statements centered on the areas you feel you need to focus. Spend a few moments with them every day and begin to internalize them. In this way you will be building a mindset that has you focused on becoming the things you wish to become.

To get you started I've put together a daily mantra of I AM statements specific to your business.

I am ready for this day. I am equipped and empowered. I am not going to let anyone steal my joy. I am focused on things that are in alignment with my goals or mission. I am focused and clear on what I need to execute today. I will not allow triggers to disrupt my plan.

Another I AM statement that I feel you should strongly consider is I AM loyal and committed. Too many loan officers' resumes are checkered with new companies that promised them the world and then couldn't deliver. They sought out lower rates, more programs, higher compensation, or more marketing. They believed their success required something externally to change. The reason for lack of success is usually not the company; it's them. A successful person will thrive and adapt no matter what the situation.

If you leave because of problems you'll just find new problems at the new company. The best time to leave is when you are already successful, you've built your disciplines and processes that keep your business sustainable, but you see that another company might be a better fit. A high-performing producer knows they have to stay in the same place longer and sell what they offer. You should only talk to a recruiter or outside company IF you have made the decision to look and you have discussed in advance with your existing company or leader exactly what you would need in order to stay. Obviously there may be times that your company is so bad you have to move. Anything else will only lead to a trap that derails your productivity and your success. Our ego will protect us from facing the cold, hard truth that we need to change and that our business plan (or lack thereof) is flawed and we might need to put in more effort. As Neil Barringham said, "The grass is greener where you water it."

Triggers and Reactions

> *"You are responsible for the energy you bring into a room."*
>
> — Oprah Winfrey —

Something we all can agree on is the mortgage business is fraught with problems. It can be frustrating because the majority of them are outside your control, i.e. low appraisals, repair issues, buyers who get cold feet, buyers who shop you when you're almost done with the loan, your ops team staff made a mistake or is behind . . . . The list goes on and on. These are what I refer to as "triggers."

A trigger is an event or thing that causes an emotional disturbance within you—fear, envy, scarcity, anger, frustration, etc. Triggers may also cause joyful reactions but most people don't need help dealing with the good stuff.

Triggers that cause negative emotions tend to cause us to react, usually in a negative way. What we need to learn is to identify our triggers upfront and then have a plan or an approach in place so that we choose to respond rather than react.

Reacting is allowing the emotion to guide you. You might yell, shut down, or send a nasty email. Responding, on the other hand, is waiting until you have assessed the situation and calmed down before you take any action.

If you see this as something that derails you the following four step process will help. I also have a trigger management strategy on my website to try if you are continuously getting "fired-up" about things.

Step 1—Become aware you are triggered.

Acknowledge that you are emotionally disturbed and have a choice to either react or respond. By emotionally disturbed I mean things like: you are angry, you are frustrated, you are sad, you are depressed, you are hopeless, you feel like quitting, or whatever it is that is affecting you in the moment. What you don't want is to have that emotion or thought become a long-term feeling.

It's important to get a handle on the difference between emotions and feelings. While the words are often used interchangeably they are actually two very different things.

Emotions are lower level responses to situations that cause a biochemical reaction in your body altering your physical state. Emotions are similar for all of us. For example, maybe you have a buyer cancels last minute and you find out that they've been shopping you and decided to go with another lender. Your emotion might be fear or anger—fear because you were counting on that money, fear because you don't know where you're next deal is coming from, fear that you won't make production. Or it might be anger that you worked so hard for nothing or that the REALTOR® didn't help keep the deal with you. Your heart might start to race, your blood pressure could go up or you might feel dizzy or nauseous.

Feelings on the other hand are long-term reactions to emotions. Think of them more as a generalized knee-jerk reaction. They are subjective and are based on your personal experiences, beliefs, and preferences. So in the example, you may have initially felt fear and anger at the borrower but if it affects your future mood or decisions then the emotion became a feeling.

Getting aware that you are not your thoughts, you are not your emotions, will help you remain detached from what your body has been patterned to do based on your past experiences. Just having some space between your emotional reaction and how you handle it will allow you to be more in control. If you don't recognize these feelings they can store up and affect your ability long-term. Watch in the following example how someone allowed a trigger to sabotage them for over a month.

I was speaking to a leadership team a few months ago and said that they are responsible for the energy they bring into the room. I said that I can tell when someone hasn't been taking care of themselves, like not getting enough sleep, because I can see it in their energy.

One of the women in the audience heard what I said differently. She heard that I can tell someone is not taking care of themselves when they are overweight. This woman was triggered—she was fired up! She couldn't get over the perception that I was somehow telling her that she wasn't taking care of herself because she was overweight and struggling with it.

With that trigger, instead of going through the next three steps, she stayed stuck in what she thought I'd said. This created a feeling for her that drove a wedge between us. She allowed that emotion to become a long-term feeling that affected her relationship and connection with me for an entire month. Once we talked about it she accepted my apology and agreed there was a major misunderstanding.

Step 2-–Identify What Preference is Not Being Met.

Triggers only occur when your preferences aren't being met. Most preferences are created by our ego and really aren't as important as they seem.

Understanding your preferences and how they can derail you will help you grow. We can learn to be more tolerant of other's faults. We can learn to be more patient. Not all of our preferences serve us. Identifying the ones that don't and eliminating them is to our benefit.

It is an ongoing journey to manage our preferences and triggers. The fewer preferences we have based on other people's actions or behaviors, the more joy we'll have in life and our business. That's not to say we can't have standards and boundaries. They simply need to be clear and agreed to by the people we do business with. Then everyone knows what to expect.

In order to prevent some of this, the first thing to do is identify the preferences that trigger you regularly. Here are a few examples of preferences:

- I prefer that there be no traffic when I have to go to a meeting or be somewhere on time

- I prefer that no one makes mistakes on my loan and there are no file delays

- I prefer that the appraisal come in at or above the sale price with no repairs

- I prefer that my house is clean and dinner is ready when I get home

- I prefer that my kids do their homework without being nagged and without needing my help after a long day

Unless you love complaining or being irritated at the same things repeatedly, you should commit to growing through your most common triggers. It is almost impossible to live an extraordinary life if you get fired up all the time, especially over the same things.

If you're finding it difficult to identify your preferences, it might help for you to keep a journal at work. Then the minute you are triggered write down what is happening and what you are feeling. Doing this provides "space" between the trigger and the action you are going to take. The difference between reacting and responding is space and awareness.

Finding your preference is uncovering what the opposite of the situation is that triggered you. For example, you get completely pissed at your processor for not requesting your docs right. Your underlying preference is that you want everyone to see you as perfect. This makes it impossible because the borrower must sign again and it has delayed closing. Although your preference is not met, you can still come out ahead by being honest. Most buyers and REALTORS® understand that we are human and make mistakes. Remembering this can be difficult when you are in the middle of it, but it is better than to rip your processor a new one and complain about him or her to the borrower and REALTOR®. Ultimately you are responsible. If you start blaming others it devalues your team.

Daily writing in a journal about what triggers me gives me space, both professionally and personally—space to see I'm emotionally triggered, space to say I could devastate and make this situation worse if I react, space to see what's the best plan of action, space to respond in a calm, positive manner. Dawson Trotman, founder of The Navigators, said it like this, *"Thoughts disentangle themselves when they pass through your fingertips."*

Step 3—Recognize Your Hallucination.

If you figure out what your hallucination is when your trigger isn't met, you will understand why it is bothering you so much. Your hallucination is the worst-case scenario that you are worried about.

The goal again is to have a plan that enables you to respond, not react and to admit you are hallucinating. Figuring it out helps make it more predictable. So many loan officers immediately go to the worst-case scenario as soon as something doesn't go as planned. They'll start thinking they're going to lose the REALTOR® forever or they need to find a new company. Or worse yet, they're going to be a total failure and not be able to provide for their family, even when the mistake or the situation had nothing to do with them and was totally outside of their control.

We all hallucinate about how bad things are. I've seen some of the clients who complain the most turn out to be the best. Mistakes are not the end of the world. In this business often our frontal lobe simulator hallucinations are ego-driven. Your brain is designed to keep you alive, not effectively handle non-life threatening situations. You need to recognize it is faulty when you are triggered. We must take a step back and remind ourselves that we are not that important. We're providing a loan. We're not on the operating table doing a heart transplant. No one is going to die if mistakes are made or something you didn't anticipate doesn't go right.

What I encourage you to do when a trigger causes you to hallucinate about all the bad things that are going to happen is to state the trigger out loud. Say, "My trigger is X because my preference of Y isn't being met, so I'm hallucinating that Z is going to happen." Just the act of saying it out loud is often enough to see the ridiculousness of what your trigger is causing you to feel.

For example: my trigger is that my son isn't doing his homework. My preference is that he completes it right after dinner before he watches TV. My hallucination is that he's never going to get into college; he's going to work at McDonalds the rest of his life and live at home.

When I say this out loud, before I say anything to my son, I can see how ridiculous I'm being. Again, I get the space I need to decide on a productive, positive response rather than reacting on my hallucination which wouldn't benefit either of us.

Step 4—Avoid or Grow.

The last step, and certainly the most important, is to decide to grow through the trigger or strive to avoid it. Let's take for example a preference for not getting stuck in traffic. When it happens you could choose to grow through it. You could use the time to raise your energy and do a mini meditation, you could be more grateful, be more present, listen to a podcast, or do something else that allows you to grow and become more patient. You could even make calls to prospects and REALTORS®.

Or you could avoid it. You could say I'm just not going to drive at this time of day, or I'm just not going to take this route because you don't think there's any way that you could grow through it. That's okay. My hope would be that you would always try to grow through it first. But we all need to give ourselves permission to draw the line when we simply can't.

Tough conversations are one example in this business where we must grow through them. They cannot be avoided. Unfortunately loan officers are generally not very good at having them.

The emotion triggered by tough conversations is often one of fear. I once received a complaint from a listing agent about a loan that wasn't closing on time. After a little bit of research I found that the loan officer had never submitted the file to underwriting because it never would have been approved. The selling agent had told him that the buyers wanted to repair their credit but neither of them had ever told the listing agent. He felt his reason was justified because he wanted to do what his REALTOR® wanted.

In my discussion with him I let him know that I felt he had a real problem telling people negative news and that he needed to grow through this. He knew he had made a mistake by not telling the listing agent. His fear of the deal falling apart made him think he could avoid having the conversation. But his avoidance hurt his personal brand with the listing agent and the company's brand as well. You have to protect both by doing the right thing every single time.

Based on this incident, this loan officer may very well decide that growing through difficult conversations is too much right now. He has had this challenge his whole life and he would have to put in a lot of effort to overcome it. Consequently he may try to avoid them by only going after strong credit borrowers: ones who don't need special assistance or hand-holding. The alternative though is much better. He can learn to grow through it and have a much more sustainable business. Everyone goes after the cream of the crop. The loan officers who learn to grow through these difficult files and want to truly help people become home owners are the loan officers who will differentiate themselves.

You must be clear though upfront about how difficult the file is and set accurate expectations. You don't need to be a hero or miracle worker in this business to succeed. Sustainability is within your grasp if you realize part of your value is being able to have clear, tough conversations with all parties.

There are five major triggers in this industry that are predictable. The very fact that they are, meaning each of you is going to experience these triggers at some point, makes it easier to have a plan in place to deal with them before they happen. What that plan consists of will depend to some extent on your preferences.

Here are the five major predictable triggers that all of you will face at one time or another. At a minimum you want to have a script ready ahead of time to ensure that you can respond appropriately, rather than react.

1. Mistakes made by loan operations or file delays; triggers losing a customer or REALTOR®—everyone has a client with a moving van outside and there will always be pressure to close faster

2. Complaints made by REALTORS® or Borrowers with your service; triggers blaming others or our staff for why these people feel this way about us, or our own insecurity about doing a good job, or the false belief that we can please everyone

3. Difficult loan file results in a file suspension or denial; triggers fear you will lose the referral source and client, and anger if you don't agree with the reasoning

4. Phones not ringing, slow activity levels; triggers scarcity, fear, stops you from doing more activity when you should increase it

5. Seeing other loan officers succeed when you aren't; triggers envy, excuses

It's so important to me to educate people on how to manage triggers because triggers are what derail people every day. When a customer calls with a problem the loan officer will often shut down. When someone isn't happy with them they tend to dwell on it. They become ineffective and their energy changes.

Negative energy is what occurs when you don't manage your triggers. No one likes to work with or be around someone who has negative energy. It causes a domino effect. Maybe you get a couple of triggers strung together. Now you've had a bad day. Then you bring it home and you're not present with your family because you're still dwelling on those triggers and negative feelings. You don't exercise and you don't take care of yourself. You might then turn to food or alcohol so that you are distracted. Without the ability to manage your triggers you end up creating a whirlwind of chaos.

The goal is to bring joyful energy into every situation. So many people believe they should just have it. I love this quote by Brendon Burchard from *The Power of Personal Responsibility*:

"The power plant doesn't have energy, it generates energy. Similarly, we don't have an attitude, we generate one."

Our energy and attitudes have to be generated every single day. Allowing our triggers to drain our positive energy and replace it with negativity and self-doubt does not serve us.

Stress Management

"I am not in charge or responsible for the wrecks others have created in their lives and I do not need to save everyone in my life."

— Brendon Burchard, *The Motivation Manifesto* —

Few non-medical professions are more stressful than the mortgage business. There are so many moving parts to closing a successful deal. Of course the central point of contact is the customer but you also have an appraiser, an underwriter, an insurance company, a mortgage insurance company, REALTORS®, a pest inspector, a home inspector, etc. All of these people with all their individual responsibilities have to come together to make a smooth transaction.

What I've seen in my many years in this business, is that the amount of pressure loan officers put on themselves to bring all of these moving parts together is not realistic. They feel responsible for every problem, every delay, and every uncooperative buyer that comes along. We put ourselves in positions of generating way more stress than is necessary. We also set expectations or timelines for others that are outside our own control.

Stress generally arises from two things:

1. Trying to control things that are beyond your reach, power, authority . . .

2. A scarcity mindset

Let's talk about wanting to have control over everything first. We think that if we have control we will have certainty. But that's simply not true. It's the very uncertain nature of this business that causes us stress. We can't tolerate that so many things are out of our hands.

The biggest aha for me was in understanding that somehow in this business we all become empaths. The problems of all the people in the loan process become our problems. We often care too much. This causes us to have a 24/7 mentality. I know many of you are still thinking about your files when you go home at night rather than being present with your family and friends. You feel like you always have to be available and that is devastating to your stress levels.

What you need to do is set boundaries. It changed my world for the better when I became more disciplined about setting and maintaining boundaries. You have to let the universe do its work and not take on the expectations of others. You must accept uncertainty and look forward to the infinite choices it will open up for you. Take a step back and say, "I don't need to take this home with me. I don't need to carry these things. I don't need to take on the stress and be weighed down with the issues of my clients or referral sources."

I think Deepak Chopra says it best in his Law of Detachment.

"In detachment lies the wisdom of uncertainty . . . in the wisdom of uncertainty lies the freedom from our past, from the known, which is the prison of past conditioning. And in our willingness to step into the unknown, the field of all possibilities, we surrender ourselves to the creative mind that orchestrates the dance of the universe."

One of the boundaries I have put in place for myself, and one that has a profound impact on how I set myself up for a successful day, is to not check my email before 8 a.m. or after 8 p.m. You may not be aware but email is a major stress producer for our industry.

A study by Professor Tom Jackson, from Loughborough University, showed 92% of the participants had elevated blood pressure and heart rates when checking their email. This is generally caused by email that is irrelevant and wasting our time or by email that requires what we feel is an immediate response. Other studies have shown that people are less productive for the rest of the day if they check their email within 60 minutes of waking up. Julie Morgenstern, the founder of Task Masters, even wrote a book titled, *Never Check Email in the Morning*.

I strongly suggest that you review your priorities, goals, and mantra instead. Focus on your I AM statements so you can step into the person you want to be for the day rather than checking email. Your value proposition should be to show up as the best "you" every day, not to always answer the phone or be available 24/7.

As I said before, the second big stressor for loan officers is a scarcity mindset. I spoke about scarcity in an earlier chapter but I sometimes feel that I can never emphasize enough how destructive this mindset is to your sustainable success.

You'll know you're in a scarcity mindset if you hear yourself saying things like: "I just don't know where I'm going to get my next deal. I don't know how I'm going to make a living. I don't know if I'm doing the right activities." A lack of clarity is what I've found to be the major contributor to a scarcity mindset. Not enough clarity in your business plan. Not enough clarity around the things you need to do every day in order to be successful.

One of the first things I do when I sit down in a coaching session with a loan officer is to ask them how many people they are receiving business from. Who are your referral partners and REALTORS®? Nine times out of ten they don't really know. They can't tell me if the referrals are coming from their database or just randomly arriving. Because they have no clarity about where they get their business, they create a significant amount of stress for themselves. There's no predictability in their financial future; just a high level of uncertainty about completing a loan and where they're going to get the next one. This stress paralyzes them. They can't take risks and they can't create opportunities because they're paralyzed by uncertainty.

So I try to help them get really clear about what their business consists of. We review every bit of business that they've done in the last year. We figure out how many repeat clients they had, how many referrals they had, how many REALTOR® referrals they had, and most importantly, how often they received them. Once they know these things they can formulate an action plan that concentrates on the major measures of output that have been shown from their past performance to have the biggest impact on their success. Think of these as levers that when pulled create certain amounts of opportunities.

By delving deep into what you have done you create a greater sense of predictability about the future of your business. You'll know what you need to accomplish. You can say I need this number of meetings every week. I need this number of qualified referral sources. You can reach a balance between certainty and uncertainty. You can stop the paralysis and open yourself up freely to handling more risk.

So from a practical standpoint what can you do to reduce stress? Try these three things:

1. Become aware of your triggers. Which of your preferences that aren't being met cause a trigger that makes you anxious, nervous, and stressed? Again, the better we learn to manage our triggers, to put space between reacting and responding, the less stress we'll have.

   Another great way to create space, when you can't write in your journal, is to breathe. Plant your feet firmly on the ground with your legs uncrossed. Take a deep breath in through your nose then let it out through your mouth. If you do this about three times, you feel your body relax allowing you to use the space to manage your trigger.

2. Create better disciplines. Put disciplines in place, boundaries, so you can run your own day not have someone else run it for you. Figure out what it is that you need to do. For example, if I do these things I will win my day.

   Loan officers by nature are on the phone or in their email far too much. Don't sit at your desk all day being an order taker. Get up and take a break every hour and shake off whatever stress might have accumulated. Take a walk. Smile at someone. You'll be amazed how simply smiling or laughing will bring you back in balance. Leave time in your day so that you can win it by being proactive about what you accomplish. Regardless of the problems that come along, you've won your day if you checked off the items on your non-negotiable activity plan.

Something that is missing in this industry is enough deadlines. Because you have so much freedom many of you choose to procrastinate. No one is telling you that you have to build x number of relationships by a certain date because your job depends on it. Many of you work at companies with no minimum production standards so no one is telling you to close x number of deals a month.

Procrastination perpetuates stress because you know you aren't doing the things you should do to win your day and build a sustainable business. I'm going to talk a lot more about procrastination in the section on sabotage. Keep in mind the importance of self-managing deadlines. Become accountable to yourself.

3. Be mindful of how you take care of yourself outside of work. To be successful you have to have an abundance of energy. You won't have the energy you need unless you're healthy. For loan officers in particular that means you need to plan to eat. Too many of you don't eat and you don't drink enough water. You sit at your desks all day long afraid that if you stop to eat, something's going to fall through the cracks. That's your ego talking again and you need to let it go. If you don't take care of yourself, eating right, drinking water, reducing stress, and exercising daily then you simply won't have the

energy you need to deal with the inevitable situations that will arise.

If you'll remember in Step 1, what we don't want is to let the emotions that are triggered to result in feelings that cause you stress. While we can't stop thoughts or emotions, we can stop the long-term suffering by controlling our feelings better. It is often the under-developed side of our ego, our lower selves, trying to make us feel important that causes stress. It pushes us to connect with people by complaining; it pushes us to connect with people by feeling stressed out. We almost feel like it's our responsibility; like if I'm going to make $300,000 a year then I'd better be stressed out doing it.

You have to let that side of ego go. You need to internalize that you are here to be filled with joy and positivity. If you have things in your life that are stressing you out, you need to carefully monitor what those are. Then you need to decide if you can grow through it, if you can remove it, or if you can avoid it. It is much more joyful to create a business when you aren't constantly stressed.

Stress can also be subconsciously caused because this is not the right business for you. I like to use a predictive index known as DISC®. There are four personality traits—Dominance, Influence, Steadiness, and Compliance. In this business it helps to have Dominance and Influence as key results in your profile. The business demands action-oriented people: people who aren't afraid of rejection; who aren't afraid to get out of their comfort zone. One of my biggest challenges as a coach is with people who think they need to know everything before they can take action. If you've been in this business any amount of time, you know that's just not possible.

If you are unwilling to get outside your comfort zone, if you are unwilling to take risks, then this may be the wrong business for you. Unless of course you have a huge database of clients with whom you already have relationships. In this case, you can comfortably just work those for more referrals. Some people can be successful starting in a bank or real estate office where business is given to them without them having to leave their comfort zone very often.

You can also find a team that supports your strengths and can generate business for you. Or you could recognize that this is your natural tendency and choose to grow through it. If you do, you'll need to get help. If you need to get over your fear of rejection then you may need to get a coach who will teach you the appropriate skills to meet with a new agent or convert someone. The skills that are needed can be taught as long as you are open to learning and trying new things and can get comfortable with getting rejected—a lot!

Becoming self-aware, recognizing your triggers, and accepting it could be completely uncomfortable to grow through them, might be exactly what you need to say, "Hey, this is not the right business for me." That's okay. It's not a sign of failure. It's a sign of success. This crazy business is not for everyone so go be authentic and find the right career for you.

Sabotage Management

"If it is important to you, you will find a way. If not, you'll find an excuse."

— Anon. —

Even if you follow all the advice in this book: adopt a new successful mindset, have your I AM statements, identify your triggers, work on a stress management plan and have a solid business plan, but you still aren't achieving at the level you want there is one more thing to explore. It is time to uncover your preferred method of self-sabotage.

If you look closely, you may have always faced this no matter if it was in sports, your career, or even in your personal life. Sabotage is where most of us get stuck. It is the gap between intention and action. For example, most of us make New Year's resolutions with every intention of keeping them. But less than 78% of us actually follow through with the action necessary to realize our intention.

The gap is the "why" we don't do the things we know we should. This is usually because we don't feel well doing them. To figure out your preferred methods of sabotage you need to review your past. You have to get curious and find repetitive patterns. Remember your brain is lazy and will do the same thing over and over if you aren't in charge. Analyze what kept you from meeting your goals. Write those things down. More than likely you'll begin to see a pattern. I would bet that your preferred methods of sabotage fall into one of the following categories.

Lack of Confidence or Self-worth—usually a lack of confidence comes from experiences that we've had in the past that we project onto the future. Maybe you oversold what could be done for a client and it backfired. Maybe you made some bad decisions because you didn't do a good enough job or stick to the boundaries you had set. Now you're afraid that the same thing is going to happen again so you avoid those situations. It holds you back from trying new things and believing you are amazing regardless of how many failures or mistakes you have had.

Lack of confidence also manifests itself when we compare ourselves to others. I once had a loan officer post that he had had an amazing month. It was interesting to see how quickly others started bashing this guy behind his back or making excuses for why they couldn't do what he had done. A state of envy or excuse making— is just your ego trying to protect you from the truth about yourself. The goal here is to combat the ego. We really are trying to create an egoless act when we do business. Our only comparison should be to the goals that we set for ourselves.

It is time to start believing in yourself and being confident no matter where you are in business or how much growth you have in front of you. You should celebrate your intentions and accept that you are a unique masterpiece. You will build so many more opportunities if you are confident in yourself. Make a commitment to building more confidence by learning more and doing things you have not done before.

Arrogance and Self-righteousness—this shows up when you feel like you don't need to go back to the basics and that you are above certain activities or even people. You're "too good" to do the foundational activities that are required to be successful.

Individuals with this sabotage trait approach the business with a fixed mindset that may cause them to appear arrogant. These individuals feel like they already know everything—a major source of sabotage. If you aren't committed to experiencing and learning and growing through new things then you are committed to plateauing at some point.

You can let this go by accepting you are no better or worse than anyone else. There is no hierarchy in life or a time when you should get away from the basics. The more entitled or arrogant you act the less people will support you. If you maintain humility and confidence together the sky is the limit for your business.

Blame and Anger—these two little demons raise their ugly heads when we are too attached to the outcome of a particular situation that doesn't work out or our preferences aren't met. You might get angry because you didn't get back the same care and attention that you gave out. This happens when you measure reciprocity one on one. When in truth, you simply need to detach yourself, knowing that you did the best you could and have faith that the good you do will come back to you; perhaps not in this particular situation but in another.

Our ego's most basic reaction is to project blame even when we are partially responsible for what happened. If you find yourself believing things are 100% someone else's fault or that it is the end of the world, it is time to take a step back. The simple truth is human beings make mistakes. In this business, the sheer number of moving parts makes this inevitable. We have to take ownership for the experiences a client has. This means we should be protecting the people that support us, even when they make a mistake, and not tearing them down. If an underwriter puts a condition on a loan that you don't happen to agree with, don't go to the customer or REALTOR® and bash him. Take the high road instead and tell the client the underwriter is responsible for selling the loan—he wouldn't' ask for something unless he needed it. Have a rational conversation with a manager and see if the condition can be removed. When we blame others or get angry we lose energy.

You may get angry because you feel entitled—you deserve success or opportunity because you're a good person or you've worked hard or you're better than someone else who already has the success you feel belongs to you. None of us are automatically entitled to anything and it's harmful for us to believe that we are. Rather, come from a place of desiring. If you simply desire rather than believe that you deserve you can keep the blame and anger triggers from wrapping you up and preventing you from doing the things you know you should be doing.

If another loan officer gets an opportunity, promotion, or special treatment and you get angry, it might be because you don't think that's fair. It's not fair that they got that builder, or they got that REALTOR® account, or they got that pricing exception, or whatever—it's not fair, that's the reason I'm not successful. The desire for life to be fair drives a lot of blame and anger. If you just focused on your own goals and what you need to create you would be in a much better position. Don't waste your time on it's not fair. Sometimes life's not fair. Get over it. If you can only accept life happens exactly as it is supposed to unfold, you will trust new opportunities will be even better for you in the future.

Time Management—or really the lack of time management is a top method of sabotage for many loan officers. We are all hardwired differently. For some, structure and discipline come easily but for others not at all. Many of you chose this profession because of the freedom it allotted you. Unfortunately, without good time management it is that very freedom that can be your downfall.

I coach loan officers to find a happy medium between total structure and total freedom. If you are 100% structured then you're a robot. On the other hand, if you lean toward 100% freedom, then you are probably a hippy from the 60s living in a commune. Where you want to be is somewhere between 10 and 90 percent.

Only you can determine where you fall on this spectrum. Can you tolerate and thrive on a day that is only 10% time managed or do you need a day that's 50% time managed in order to be successful. Everyone needs to find their own equilibrium—there is no right or wrong answer. What is important is that you understand the output levels that you need to hit each day in order to build a sustainable business. Then you can create a business plan that includes the appropriate amount of time management to get those things done. You want to be certain that you aren't wasting time on things that are not big priorities.

I encourage loan officers to eat three frogs before they get into reactive mode like responding to email. If you're not familiar with the concept, it's based on a story by Mark Twain. Mr. Twain said you should start each day by eating a live frog. If you do, you'll have the satisfaction of knowing that eating that frog is probably the worst thing that will happen to you today. Brian Tracy, a motivation and time management guru, took this concept and wrote a book called *Eat that Frog*.

The frog represents the biggest, ugliest, most important, and maybe most undesirable task that you need to accomplish. These are often the tasks we procrastinate on because they're uncomfortable or difficult. I'm sure you know what they are for you. Failure to eat the "frogs" on your list will have consequences to your business. So do the hardest or the worst first. Then enjoy the freedom knowing that you've stayed fully committed to your plan.

Laziness—defined as the quality of being unwilling to work or use energy. But that's not how it applies here as a sabotage mechanism. Laziness in this context actually results because people have too much to do. They know what they should be doing but aren't doing it. The sheer quantity of what they need to accomplish overwhelms them. They feel like they can't get anywhere. They don't know where to start so they don't. And the longer they wait to start, the harder it is.

They avoid doing what needs to be done by turning to television or Facebook or a million other unimportant tasks. They begin to make excuses and refuse to acknowledge their own role in the story.

If you feel like laziness may be one of your preferred methods of sabotage I would encourage you to ask yourself these questions: what are you trying to avoid, and what do you think you're going to gain by avoiding it and distracting yourself? Then step back and look at all the time you spent watching television, surfing the web, texting, etc. and make a list of all the things you've created from those activities. My guess is you won't be able to put anything on that list. There is no sustainable joy or progress that comes from those activities and there certainly isn't any sustainable business or financial success that comes from them.

I'm not saying that you can never have any downtime watching TV, gaming, or reading a fiction book. But I am suggesting that you need to build those activities into your plan after you have done your daily disciplines. You need to give yourself permission to do them with a plan that includes exactly how much time you feel you can be distracted by these things and still accomplish what you need to accomplish. The goal is to remove conflict and not beat yourself up for relaxing.

Once you've limited your distractions you'll need to get past the feeling of being overwhelmed. Often it helps to stop looking at the enormity of what needs to be done and instead break each project down into small pieces. Start tackling each of those small pieces and celebrate your success when you've accomplished them. Before you know it, the big project will be complete too.

Excuse Making

> *"Excuses are the nails used to*
> *build a house of failure."*
> — Jim Rohn, Business Philosopher —

We all do it and we've been doing it most of our lives. Think back to the example of "the dog ate my homework." Excuses are a mechanism we use to ensure that people will still like us, even though we often have deliberately made a choice not to follow through on a personal commitment. Sometimes the very person we are trying to convince to still like us, is us. It is super easy to make excuses if we lack the discipline needed to do things even when we don't feel like it.

One of the methods I teach loan officers is to become aware of your excuse making voice. Recognize it as something separate from who you really are. For example, maybe one of your goals is to go to the gym on Tuesdays. Tuesday rolls around and you begin to feel like maybe you won't go. You say in your head, "Oh well, I can go tomorrow and double the amount of time."

You must recognize this is your excuse making voice and is not who you really are. This is not the person who set your goals—it's the voice who's just making excuses. Check the excuses you make against the goals you created and you will find major common ones you probably use daily.

Three of the most common excuses I hear in this business are:

1. It's not a big deal if I don't follow through on a commitment I gave a client or REALTOR®. I can just apologize and do it later. It's as if you think it will be easier sometime in the future.

2. I will call the borrower or REALTOR® with difficult news later. It will be easier to deal with tomorrow. Maybe you have convinced yourself it might just go away.

3. I will start working on my activities tomorrow or next week when I am more prepared and have more energy.

I encourage you to list out your top excuses in business for not doing what you are supposed to do. It is helpful to do them in your personal life as well because this is commonly why we don't live the life we want. This way, when you make an excuse, you'll be able to see the pattern of the ones that happen time and again. You'll begin to recognize them as a common theme that isn't getting you anywhere in your business.

Fear—aka False Evidence Appearing Real. The only way to get past fear is to understand where it comes from and be aware of it when it hits you. Fear can show up as a pit in your stomach or cause a major physical disruption. Most of our fear originates from something that happened in our past or something that someone in our life modeled for us. You'll need to get really curious to try and identify the source.

You should ask yourself questions like: When's the first time you remember being afraid? When is the first time you felt rejected? When is the first time you felt I can't fail because I'm hallucinating it will be the end of the world if I do? Sometimes finding the source makes it easier to realize how silly your fear is. There is no appropriate fear, once you are an adult, other than when you fear for your life. You have to make a decision to let fear go in this business.

I was in my early 20s when I started my career as a loan officer. I obviously didn't have much experience so it was difficult calling on real estate agents. I popped into one REALTOR'S® office who told me in a nonchalant way that he wouldn't do business with me because he felt like I would only be doing this for a few years. He suggested I'd quit to have children. He wanted to know what my husband did and then suggested that I didn't need to make money, further questioning my commitment. He made me feel like I wouldn't be successful with many REALTORS® because of my age and gender.

My instant reaction was to feel rejection that no one would have confidence in me because of my age. I also had fear I would never find enough REALTORS® to do business with. It could have stopped me from sticking to my plan of calling on ten REALTORS® a week. Fortunately, I powered through this fear and kept at it. I became aware that I had to accept rejection quickly and move on. I had to let go of everyone liking me and get used to strange conversations.

His comments inspired me to create a vision for my perfect REALTOR® that didn't include working with people that were a. going to objectify me, or b. not take me seriously. I realized that 95% of the REALTORS® I wanted to work with were women between the ages of 45 and 60. If it's possible to find humor in these situations we should. It will help us to put the fear behind and move on.

There is importance in trial and error. We need to fail in order to learn to do things differently. We don't need to be afraid to fail or to be rejected. One of the most effective things you can do is to turn your fears into a test. Say for example you need to meet with five REALTORS®. Decide upfront that with two of them you're going to take one approach, with two more you'll take a different approach, and with the last one you're just going to wing it.

After the meetings analyze what success you had with those five REALTORS®. Okay, I got rejected by two of them when I did this or that, but was successful or partially successful when I did this. In this scenario you're just testing and learning. There's no such thing as rejection—you're just trying to get the right blueprint.

Unfortunately it's not always fear of failure that triggers sabotaging mechanisms. Sometimes it's the fear of success. Remember those lenders who made a fortune in 2008 and then lost it all? They now associate that success with loss. They're afraid to go forward and do it again.

Understanding where our fear originates will help us to understand how it is impacting our current decisions. Most likely it is keeping us locked in our comfort zone, preventing us from moving out into the world. Once again, be aware that joy, and sustainable success, only happen when you are outside your comfort zone.

Procrastination—here's the funny thing about procrastinators—they're usually the ones who make "to do" lists and then don't do any of it. Then they beat themselves up for not doing it. Procrastinators spend too much time making lists and avoid taking action when they should be taking action.

There is a YouTube video on procrastination by Tim Urban that I would encourage you to watch. Here's the URL: https://www.youtube.com/watch?v=arj7oStGLkU

Tim talks about the three "characters" within the procrastinator's brain. The first is the Rational Decision Maker. He's the one that knows what needs to be done and has the will to get it done. The second is the Instant Gratification Monkey. The IGM only cares about doing things that are fun and easy. He has more power than the Rational Decision Maker so he takes control and steers the procrastinator to waste time doing fun stuff like surfing the internet, partying, watching TV, etc. The only thing that the monkey is afraid of is The Panic Monster.

The Panic Monster comes out when deadlines get too close, when there is fear of public embarrassment, or when the procrastinator's career is at risk. When The Panic Monster arrives the monkey gives control back to the Rational Decision Maker who has to scramble to save the day.

Unfortunately for loan officers, The Panic Monster rarely makes an appearance because we rarely have set deadlines except for contingency removal or close of escrow dates. Therefore it's easy for us to procrastinate indefinitely. Subconsciously though, we know we should be doing the things that need to get done; those mundane things like making calls, going to open houses, updating our database, working our plan. It's this subconscious guilt about inaction that leads to long-term unhappiness and regrets. It makes us feel like a spectator in our own lives.

To combat procrastination you first need to identify the distractions that are keeping you from doing things. Is your environment supporting your focus? For example, do you share an office with someone who wants to talk all the time? Do you always have your TV tuned to ESPN or Facebook in the background?

Or are you creating the distractions yourself? Because if you really don't want to do something it's going to be hard for you to stay focused. If you know because you've got a plan that there are things you need to do, then set your own deadlines to get them done. Don't let the Instant Gratification Monkey steal your joy and your success.

Perfectionism

> *"Perfectionism is not a quest for the best.*
> *It is a pursuit of the worst in ourselves,*
> *the part that tells us that nothing*
> *we do will ever be good enough . . ."*
>
> — Julia Cameron —

I mentioned earlier that to be successful in this business it helps to be a high D on the DISC® predictive index. High Drivers are out there looking for significance. They are often perfectionists without even realizing it.

Part of the issue is the myth that perfectionism is a desire to be perfect. It is not. Perfectionism is the belief that you are only good if someone else sees you that way. In essence, a perfectionist cares more about other people's perceptions than they care about their own.

Perfectionism was one of my top preferred methods of sabotage. From a very early age I felt like I wanted to be the smartest, I wanted to be the most popular, I wanted to be the teacher's pet, I wanted to be this, and I wanted to be that. But it wasn't that I truly wanted any of those things. What I wanted was for everyone else to believe I was those things. There's a big difference between how you feel about yourself and wanting others to see you as perfect.

Perfectionism causes people to wait. They are so worried that they're going to be embarrassed, or they're going to fail, or it's not going to be good enough that they wait to take action until the situation is perfect. A perfect situation rarely happens so nothing gets done. In fact, a lot of times a perfectionist will take an all or nothing approach. If they can't be absolutely amazing for everyone else to see then they won't do it at all.

If you fall into the perfectionist trap like I did, the first thing you need to recognize is that nobody cares. It's an illusion if you think that they do. No one spends as much time thinking about you as you. No one cares if you're "perfect." They're worried about their own issues and their own performance. You need to not let it matter what other's think. It matters what you think. You can be a good person who feels great about what you are doing. You can be of service, you can make an impact on people's lives but you cannot, and should not, live life through other people's eyes. If this is a challenge for you, check out Brené Brown's work in *The Gifts of Imperfection*. She was instrumental to me in overcoming some of my issues in this area.

Thinking too Much—You've heard of paralysis by analysis, right? Well in the mortgage industry this is especially true. Mortgage is a head-game where you are asked to think critically a lot. If you have a deal to get done, it's important to sit down and think through the steps that need to occur. It's helpful to put an action plan together to ensure that nothing falls through the cracks.

What's not helpful is if you spend too much time over-thinking the process; trying to plan for every possibility, for every eventuality. This type of thinking leads to anxiousness, regret, and worry. You start to hallucinate again about what people will think of you if things don't go 100% right.

You might also be spending too much time thinking about building your business. You might be consumed with reading books (this one excluded of course) on the subject, talking to colleagues, or going to seminars on best practices. You spend so much time thinking about it that you don't take action. You don't take the steps necessary to build a sustainable business. You get lost in trying to find the Holy Grail or chasing elephants instead of sticking to simple basics.

Instead what you should be doing is accepting the uncertainty of the future. You need to have goals and a plan to achieve them but you can't waste time trying to hypothesize about what might happen. Looking to predict the future is an exercise in futility designed to keep you from acting which effectively sabotages your success.

If you've got a big deal going and there's an issue, don't spend all day thinking about it. Look at the file, then shut it, and go home to be present with your family and friends. Let your subconscious mind do the heavy lifting and solve it for you while you sleep or when you're in the shower. Don't try to force an answer through conscious thought.

This is another area where I encourage you to journal. If you're scared shitless about something, write it down and then let it go. You'll be amazed at how often just writing something down will help you to see it for what it is.

I wish I could say that once you've identified your preferred methods of sabotage it is then easy to deal with and eliminate them. It's not. Sabotage management is an ongoing process. It takes a commitment to being constantly aware of your goals and the discipline to determine whether or not you are meeting them. It must become part of your business execution plan. I'll talk more about this in Level 3.

Commitment to Discipline

I've talked several times about having discipline. Discipline and habits are what all high performers have in common. It is one of the keys to building a strong foundation. Discipline allows you to sink your footers deep.

Discipline is hard. Nobody really feels like eating carrots and kale to stay healthy. Nobody really feels like going out and knocking on doors or making cold calls to REALTORS®. Nobody really feels like being rejected 98% of the time which is what happens in this business. It's not fun. It never will be fun.

This is why so many of us wait to be motivated before we act. Motivation, remember, is doing what needs to be done when we want to do it. You need to let go of that notion. You're not going to wake up every morning wanting to do the mundane, difficult tasks that need to be done. But you keep hoping that you will. And then you beat yourself up when you don't do what you know you should. You get caught in this perpetual loop that always ends in you being disappointed in yourself. You have to be able to love yourself before you can love and be of service to others. You must walk away from the notion of motivation.

What you need to do instead is rely on discipline. Don't get me wrong. I love motivation. I wish we could all be more motivated. But in this business discipline is what gets you through. Discipline is doing what needs to be done when it needs to be done when we **don't want** to do it. Discipline is eating those frogs. Relying on discipline rather than motivation will in fact take you where you want to be.

For example, no matter what I get up at 6 a.m. I spend an hour on mindset, on prayer, on other things that I know are going to put me in a state of joy. I need to be in this state because I'm attacked daily—things come at me. I'm running a sales team and supporting other people. I've got to be in a state where nobody steals my joy. Are you in that state? If not, then you need to get yourself there.

This must be a part of your new you. You must be disciplined to create a sustainable business.

> *"We must all suffer from one of two pains: the pain of discipline or the pain of regret. The difference is discipline weighs ounces while regret weighs tons."*
> — Jim Rohn —

Accountability

> *"Accountability breeds response-ability."*
> — Stephen Covey —

Being in a commissioned based world with all the freedom that entails makes it hard to remain accountable if the only person you're accountable is to yourself. You need to give permission to someone else to hold you accountable.

Humans do better with coaches. We need coaches; we need leadership to stay on track. We need someone we trust to hold our feet to the fire. We need someone to be our Panic Monster. Otherwise our humanness, our Instant Gratification Monkey, may lead us in the wrong direction. I have a business coach and a life coach. I can't imagine having the success I've had without them.

If your workplace doesn't offer coaching as one of your benefits, then hire your own. Or find a colleague, mentor, or friend that you trust to do the job. It has to be someone who is immune to your excuses and the other preferred methods of sabotage that you'll try.

If you think back to the chapter on mindset—our goal is to be responsive not reactive. Reactivity sabotages our business, responsiveness moves it forward. An account-ability partner will help you maintain the discipline you need to get things done. They'll allow you to create the space you need to be responsive.

Your new mindset and tools on managing stress, triggers, and self-sabotage are the most important parts of your success. You will not be able to take your business to the next level unless you are ready to. You will only multiply problems and stress if you have a plan to increase your business without being emotion-ally intelligent enough to handle more challenges and problems. As you build your plan in Level 2 keep in mind that you need to continuously focus on growing so you can adapt to any market changes and also inspire your REALTORS® to do the same.

LEVEL 2
THE PLAN

—

"Don't be afraid of the space between your dreams and reality. If you can dream it, you can make it so."

— Belva Davis —

Now that you've built your foundation with deep, strong footers it's time to turn to framing. Framing your foundation is what will give it shape and dimension. To do this we must first devise a vision. Then we create realistic goals and a business plan to accomplish our vision. Lastly, we put the processes, procedures, and business systems in place to ensure we can carry out our plan and achieve our goals.

According to www.businessdictionary.com, a vision statement is *an aspirational description of what an organization would like to achieve or accomplish in the mid-term or long-term future. It is intended to serve as a clear guide for choosing current and future courses of action.*

In this case the organization is you. You must have clarity around your life and your business if you want to develop sustained joy. All the top performers, regardless of industry, have a habit of being clear about their vision. Your vision statement should help you be more intentional about how you live your life and how you work your business.

Before deciding on your personal vision, ask yourself the following questions:

- Who do you want to be?
- Where do you want your business to be in five or ten years?
- How do you want to feel?

The keys to creating a compelling vision statement are to dream big and use concise language. It is a living, breathing testament to how you will go about your day so it should be written in present tense. Here are some condensed examples of vision statements by companies you know:

Disney—To make people happy.

Microsoft—Empower every person and every organization on the planet to achieve more.

Coca Cola—Being a responsible global citizen that makes a difference.

You can create a short one or make it detailed. I like to focus on the impact I make in other's lives and how I feel doing it. My vision statement for my business before was: To impact the lives of the clients and REALTORS® I serve by providing top notch service while maintaining joy and balance. Now that I no longer originate it is: With an open heart I will fearlessly share love and wisdom with the world creating more joy and less suffering.

There is no right or wrong way to write a vision statement. It just has to be in alignment with the overall life you want to lead. Joy has special importance for me both personally and professionally. If I cannot do something with joy, I won't do it. The major thing is that once it's written, it resonates with you. If you don't get excited every time you read it, then it isn't truly your vision.

I've included a form here for you to use to record your vision statement and the goals and questions we'll design later in this chapter. It's important to have everything in one place so it's easy to review. The more often you review, the deeper it will go, and the easier it will be for you to act consistently in alignment with your vision. Think of it as your purpose for your business.

Business Vision

_____

_____

_____

_____

_____

Goals and Values:

Top 5 Values	Top 5 Goals	Away from Values

Daily Questions

1. _____

2. _____

3. _____

Goals

*"Setting goals is the first step in turning
the invisible into the visible."*

— Tony Robbins —

I like to believe that everyone's ultimate vision is to live an extraordinary life. I define extraordinary as doing what you love and loving how you do it. It is not defined by the amount of money you make or number of loans you fund. The greatest tool I've found for doing this is creating tangible goals. Goal setting propels your vision forward. When you're defining what an extraordinary life looks like you're maximizing the resources that you have: your time, your skills, your knowledge, and your passion so you can make the most of your life and feel more fulfilled about what you're doing.

I started practicing goal planning in the late 90s after attending several events that all led me to believe it was the key to personal success and happiness. I truly believe it gave me an edge over others that didn't have goals in my market.

When you write out your goals, you're creating an external representation of your internal desires and reinforcing their value. Setting tangible goals allows you to break those big dreams into bite-size, achievable steps.

And most important, goals hold you accountable. They get you out of the "if only" rut that steals so much of your joy and happiness: if only I made more money, if only I lost this weight, if only my business were thriving, then I'd be happy. Often people don't know they're leading an extraordinary life because they have so many "if onlys" that they become trapped in a hamster wheel. There's always another if only. Tangible goals help you to see and celebrate your successes.

Part of goal planning is becoming that person who is joyful and happy today even though you haven't yet achieved all you may want. It needs to be an overall look at your entire life, not just the business piece. You have to find a balance in what you do because we all have multiple priorities in our life. If all you do is set goals for your business then you may be unconsciously sabotaging yourself if those goals are in conflict with your vision for your family, your relationships, or your personal development.

Another habit of top performing individuals is that they make it a goal to cultivate more energy. If your goals are in conflict with how much energy you have, you are not likely to reach them. It will take more energy if you want to accomplish more than what you have in the past. When I coach loan officers on goal setting I always talk with them about cultivating more energy as part of their plan so they don't lose steam and end up beating themselves up. You have to prioritize creating energy in your goals by taking care of your body and health and also getting enough downtime to recharge. The energy you bring to each day is a major indicator of being able to live an extraordinary life and build a sustainable business.

Before you begin to write your goals go back to what you learned in Level 1 and assess your current mindset. Is it in alignment with your vision? Are you becoming the person you want to be or are you in a rut? Here's my definition of a rut: you wake up in the morning and you're not excited to start your day and when you go to sleep at night you're not grateful for the day you had. Ninety-nine percent of people, according to my definition, are in a rut. It takes time and effort to feel this way. It is much easier to suffer and feel exhausted.

Assuming your vision is to be successful, impact more lives by what you do and how you do it, and lead an extraordinary life then you should at a minimum have a mindset that is: growth minded, purpose driven, value driven, and one that is focused on abundance and not scarcity. If you're not quite there yet, and not many of us are, your goal setting should include specific goals to address these issues in addition to those related to your business.

Goal Setting Process

The method I use to do goal planning is a simple four step process:

1. **Make a commitment.** Too many people write down goals and then never follow through on them. Just like those New Year's resolutions that last only a week or two. If you are serious about

creating an extraordinary life and building a sustainable business you must be committed to attaining the goals you set for yourself. You have to say, "for the next 3 months, 6 months, 12 months, I'm going to entrench myself in living this goal." You are committed to sitting down with them every single day, reviewing them and checking in with yourself to see if you're getting closer to or farther away from what you want to achieve. That's why the Vision Statement form also contains space for your top five goals.

2. **Identify what you really want.** Get really clear about this. What do you want to achieve? What types of people do you want to work with? How do you want to feel? What do you want to change in your mindset or in your sabotaging behaviors? What outputs or outcomes are desired? (For a loan officer these might be number of credit pulls, pre-approvals, piped or funded loans—all things that can be measured).

3. **Recognizing why you want it.** If you are going to stay committed you have to understand why you want the things you want. Most people will say something like, "Well, I want to make $20,000 a month." That's great but I push them farther to get to the underlying reason why $20,000 is important. What does it mean to make that money? Well it could mean they can save money for retirement so they can live the life they want, or it might mean

being able to put their children through college, or maybe it allows them to take the vacations they've always wanted, or pay off debt that's been holding them back. The deeper you can get into the "why" of the wanting, the more leverage you'll have and the more committed you will be to following through on the activities necessary to accomplish your goals. Be careful that fear is not your leverage.

4. **Create a plan in order to achieve them.** Plain and simple, if you don't plan your life, it will be controlled by other demands. If you didn't create goals last year, take a look back. What results did you or didn't you accomplish and how did it affect you? Chances are you won't be able to quantify it. Oh sure, you may know your numbers but do you really know how you achieved them? Do you know what your conversion rates were and where all your business came from? If you were successful do you know how to duplicate it going forward, and if you weren't, do you know what needs to change?

Unless we have tangible results from the activities we engaged in—whether it's spending time on Facebook, cultivating new business relationships, or working our database—our brain will not remember why it's supposed to keep doing these things. That's why it's so important to be disciplined about setting our goals and executing a plan to obtain them.

But as we talked about earlier, it's not enough to just set goals. They need to be the right goals. They need to be

S.M.A.R.T. This acronym was first written down in November, 1981 by consultant George T. Doran in a paper he published entitled, "There's a S.M.A.R.T. Way to Write Management Goals and Objectives." It stands for: Specific, Measurable, Action Oriented, Realistic, and Time Sensitive. Each goal should be written with these five things in mind.

Specific: getting exceptionally clear about what you are going to accomplish

Measurable: Remember the adage—inspect what you expect. You are trying to build feelings of success. You need to set goals that allow you to see the progress you are making.

I like to put my mindset goals on a spectrum of one to ten where ten is the desired result. Take the goal of feeling abundance for example. Imagine a spectrum where scarcity is a one and total feeling of abundance is a ten. Every day you can assess where you are on that scale. Maybe you're a four today. You are still worried about being able to pay your bills. If some deals don't close you get anxiety when you go to the grocery store and swipe your debit card, even though you know that there's money in your account. Overtime as you build up a reserve account, when you get to where you're feeling a seven or an eight, you will know that your mindset has shifted and you have grown through scarcity. You've earmarked money for groceries and vacations and you're supposed to be spending money on these things.

Another example might be a goal of resilience where one is being not resilient at all, losing my shit every single day, and ten being everything just rolls off me like a duck. It's all about asking daily, where am I today? Where am I trying to move myself on that needle?

Action Oriented: Nothing gets done if you don't take action. Contrary to information found in *The Secret* you can't wish it and it will come. That's not to say that a golden egg will never land in your lap, but you'll have far more eggs if you actively go out and collect them.

Realistic: It helps to make sure your goals are realistic before you start taking action on them. For example, new loan officers shouldn't set a goal to fund $25,000,000 in their first year. There's a learning curve involved. They need to learn the business—what works and what doesn't. And referral sources take time to develop. When your goals are unrealistic your brain knows it. You'll only end up in a place of excuse making and self-sabotage.

Time Sensitive: If something is going to get accomplished it must have a deadline. Remember the Instant Gratification Monkey? We all need Panic Monsters to get important things done. It's just part of human behavior. So recognize that our business doesn't have many deadlines. We need to set them and be committed to keeping them.

Making Your Goals Work

In order to maintain balance and not allow your goals to conflict with each other, it helps to put them in four categories: Business, Financial, Health, and Family/Relationships. You should have a couple of short and long-term goals in each category.

You should create a couple short-term (3 months) and a couple long-term (12 months) goals for each category. Next identify the top action steps you're going to take to accomplish each goal. Then finally, you'll want to identify what you want to avoid the most and the top way that you typically sabotage yourself in meeting this goal.

These are what I call "away values." They are things you are patterned to do that no longer serve you. I first came across this term when studying NLP—Neuro Linguistic Programming—a method of teaching your conscious mind the language of your unconscious mind—taught by the Empowerment Partnership. Examples of away values would be passivity, perfectionism, judgement—any of your sabotage methods.

For business one of my top away values is being passive. I want to really be able to speak up and move forward, not just swallow whatever I'm thinking in fear others won't agree. The perfectionism I battle makes me worry sometimes about how I will be viewed by others. I worry too much about everyone liking me, which is impossible in this business. It can make me passive at times. I need to hold others accountable or take the massive action I need to.

I like to keep all of my goals in one place so I can easily review them often. I use a journal to do this. Each goal has its own page. Every morning I wake up, take out my journal and review all my I AM statements, my vision, my values (both those I want to keep and those I want to eliminate), and my goals. I redo my goals every six months since that's about what my journal will hold.

I'm going to reiterate the importance of reviewing your goals every day. If you do so, you'll drive the concepts of what you want to accomplish deeper into your subconscious and conscious mind so they become more patterned. Contrary to popular opinion, it's not about reprogramming your brain; it's about programming it for the first time. Your brain wants to take the path of least resistance so it will react based on past experience. It is so lazy! But if you set your goals deeper with really great intention, then your brain will react with that intent.

For example, let's say someone's goal in business is to be more open-minded and connected. Maybe it's because they realize they're an asshole—they have a habit of sending nasty emails to people and have combative relationships whether it's a referral partner, a processor, or a client. When they enter into territory where something goes wrong, their natural response, their path of least resistance, is to be a jerk because they've always acted this way. If they looked at their goals and their away values in the morning, they'd be more intentional that day in terms of not being a jerk. If their goal is to be a kinder person, they can decide in the morning ways they could do that. They need to ask themselves, how can I practice being more kind? How can I dedicate five minutes every morning just to kindness? Perhaps they could send a gratitude email to every person who made a difference to them the previous day.

If you are rude or condescending, you will minimize the amount of success you have in this business. People will not work as hard for you as they do for people who are kind and grateful. It may seem logical to blow up at people that make mistakes because they did something wrong but their humanness will guide them to not work as hard for you in the future. Like the restaurant employee that might spit in someone's food for complaining and sending food back, escrow officers, underwriters, processors, and funders may make a file tougher than it needs to be. If you are smart you will learn to be more strategic about always being kind even when problems arise.

I realize not everyone likes to journal. It doesn't really matter what form you use to keep your goals as long as they are easy to access and you commit to a daily morning review. Some of the loan officers I work with have them set up as their screen saver. Others have written them on their bathroom mirror or a poster board at work. I'm sure someone has even made them into an audio recording they can listen to each day. You need to choose whatever works for you and keeps you closer to the life you want to live.

But for those of you who may still be feeling a bit overwhelmed, I've devised a simple form for you to get started:

Goals and Action Steps

	Short Term: 3 months	Long Term: 1 year	Top Action Steps: 3 months	Top Action Steps: 1 year	What I want to avoid most and the top ways I sabotage myself.
Business			1. 2. 3.	1. 2. 3.	
Financial			1. 2. 3.	1. 2. 3.	
Health/Personal			1. 2. 3.	1. 2. 3.	
Family			1. 2. 3.	1. 2. 3.	

Once you've written down your goals and you're comfortable that they are realistic and not in conflict with each other, I DON'T want you to start action right away. I always recommend that you sit with these goals and let them marinate a bit. You could cook a steak as soon as you bring it home, but if you marinate it for a while it's probably going to taste better. I recommend that you let your goals marinate for a week. Do them once and put them away. Then come back a week later and reevaluate them. Although you haven't looked at them or acted on them, subconsciously your mind will have been thinking about them.

Ask yourself these questions:

Are these really my goals or what is expected of me from my family, my boss, society, or anyone else?

If you can't answer yes, then the goal is not a good goal and you are setting yourself up for failure. If the goal isn't coming from your higher purpose, your desire, or what you envision for your life, then you will be lacking the leverage and the dedication required to take the actions that will get you there.

Are these goals aligned with my core values?

For example, if you know you have a core value of balance but you're working 60 hours a week to reach an unrealistic business goal, then those are going to be in conflict with each other. You're not going to have the time to nurture relationships if you're a workaholic.

I coached a manager a while back that never felt great about what they were accomplishing, even though they were highly successful compared to our company's standards. When we sat down and did a core values exercise it became clear that one of his chief values was balance. He had a deep desire to coach his son's football team but he'd never been able to because he was working until 7 p.m. every night. So we decided to set a goal that he would coach the next season. We then came up with the action steps he needed to take to accomplish this goal without jeopardizing success in other areas of his life. Years later he has achieved more balance and business success AND has coached his son for three years.

I strongly recommend that you get clear on your value system even before you put together your vision. Identify the top five values for your business and for your life. There is space on the Vision Statement form for this. For me the top driving business values are growth, innovation, relationships, integrity, and gratitude. Every day without question that's what I look at, that's what I coach to. If I'm in a meeting or sharing messages with my team, it's always in alignment with one of those top five values.

How much time do you have to allocate to your goals?

Do you actually have enough time in your day, week, or month to accomplish all your goals? For example, if you have a health goal of running a marathon and you have a business goal of funding $50,000,000, how are you going to fit it all in? Will you be able to prioritize your time to accomplish both? You want to make sure that the goals you set are achievable given that there are only 1,440 minutes in every day and part of that time you need to sleep.

Does this goal provide the feeling or outcome you want to achieve and will it sustain you long-term?

I always tell my loan officers, if your goals aren't life or death, don't write them down. You should approach goal setting like, "No matter what I will fund $50 million, or I will have 20 referral sources that are giving me business, or I want to get in the best shape of my entire life and I'm going to stop at nothing to get it done! Don't approach goal planning with just a lighthearted, "Oh it would be fabulous if I were able to do that." Not taking action on the goals you set is more devastating to your psyche than if you didn't set them at all.

Disciplines/Habits/Rituals

No one reaches their goals by simply writing them down. No one reaches their goals by acting on them occasionally. To reach your goals you must have disciplines, habits, and rituals. In assessing you goals ask yourself, what daily disciplines do I need to adopt?

Your goals should have you dreaming big. They should be more than you accomplished before, taking into consideration new market conditions. But that can make them seem overwhelming. You need to break the goals down into bite-size action steps that you can take to accomplish them.

For example, to meet your goal of having 20 Referring REALTORS® within six months, you may need to meet with at least two real estate agents every single day. What disciplines are you going to need in order to this? For starters you're going to have to make enough phone calls every day to generate two meetings.

Once you find the daily disciplines needed for each goal you will start to see the compound effect of all your activity. It is usually the little things you do every day that make a difference in building a sustainable business.

In addition to developing the right disciplines and doing them consistently, it is also important to understand what habits you have that might get in the way of accomplishing your goals. To discover what they are you need to get curious about who you've been in the past. Habits are hard to break but super simple to form, particularly if they are bad habits that satisfy the Instant Gratification Monkey. Maybe one of your habits has been to eat ice cream every night before bed. If your goal is to lose weight you're going to have to give up this habit. Recognizing the habits that might keep you from achieving your goal and controlling or eliminating them is critical in avoiding self-sabotaging behavior.

Now that you have your goals reevaluated and set, and you've identified the disciplines you need and the habits you either need to break or to form, it's time to put together an action plan.

The first piece of your plan is to strategize about who you may need to help you. If there are people in your life who are encouraging your bad habits then you may need to talk with them about how you're trying to change and ask them to support you. You may realize that you can't go it alone and need to hire a coach who will help you stay accountable to the goals that you set. Or maybe you need to speak with your manager about how they can help you to stay on task.

It helps if you create a daily, weekly, and monthly activity planner. This is not a "to do" list, this is your commitment plan. If one of your disciplines is to make 20 real estate agent calls a week then schedule those calls into your weekly plan or calendar. Perhaps you make ten calls each on Tuesdays and Thursdays. No matter what—on Tuesday and Thursday according to your planner you are going to be on the phone until you've completed those ten calls.

Like everything else, the commitment plan you create works best if you keep it in front of you—on your wall at work or on your computer or in your calendar. Every day, whenever you look at them, remember your leverage and why you committed to it. Each week you should evaluate the results you received so your brain is rewarded. This helps formulate conversion rates as well which are critical in re-assessing what you need to do to reach your goals. I am always asking myself, "Am I getting closer or further away from accomplishing my goals?" so that I can make quick adjustments to my daily disciplines if needed.

It's okay to not always be moving forward. Life does often get in the way. But just because you fall behind doesn't mean you should give up. Reset your plan and start again. You need to be comfortable that you can keep starting over as often as is necessary if you hit a roadblock or bump. Every day you can start new. If you had a bad day yesterday, don't let that bad day turn into two bad days, or three bad days.

Break the cycle of only starting again on Monday. If you don't, you'll waste too much time beating yourself up about the things that aren't getting done and just keep procrastinating. Then you'll have to self-soothe with laziness or distractions. Part of the reason we set goals is to get out of this destructive behavior. I'm a firm believer that we ought to have a disaster preparedness plan for when we get off track with our goals. Living on the west coast I'm fairly certain that an earthquake isn't going to hit but I should have a plan for it in the event it does. The same is true for reaching your goals. Life is outside of our control. You can't avoid problems, so create a quick, easy disaster preparedness plan that you can activate if you get thrown off and you're just not feeling it?

When I feel I'm entering into a self-sabotaging shit storm, I have a life coach that I call immediately. I usually see her every other week but when my circus monkeys come to town she knows I'll be calling. I have to stop and take a break. I'm not going to make any big decisions about my business or my life at these times. I have a plan that when I get into this season, and it is just a season, I'm going to have more solitude and get support from the people whose opinions I value.

So many loan officers, when they start to self-sabotage, turn on the company and the people that supported them. They focus on the negatives of the company, they want to quit their job, or distract themselves heavily perhaps by drinking alcohol. Their brains go immediately to what they know—I'm going to lose or I can't handle this, I'm going to walk away, go someplace else, this is too hard. Having the awareness to know you are creating your own suffering is critical. You need to get happy in spite of the problem and crisis at hand before you make any life decisions.

You may be wondering, if it's that easy, if we can simply start over, why isn't everybody doing it? Usually it's because of the limiting beliefs that we have or the stories that we tell ourselves. We don't hold ourselves accountable. We have thoughts like; if I'm successful then everyone is always going to expect me to be successful. Think again about how you allow yourself to make excuses and why. Go back to the self-sabotaging work that you did in Level 1. Have you seriously identified them and how they align with jeopardizing your goals?

Most people want to sweep them under the rug and pretend they don't exist.

I don't believe in that approach. I'm one of the few coaches who want to talk more about your away from values and your self-sabotage than the goals you have. I want the away from values on your goal sheet and in front of you every single day. That's why there's a column specifically for them. I recommend that you spend five minutes every day dealing with your away from values. What does that mean? If, for example, you're a procrastinator then I want you to spend five minutes every day googling or reading and doing research on how to overcome procrastination. If you're not resilient then spend five minutes researching how to be more resilient. Again, being consistent in this practice is a key to reducing or eliminating those values that no longer serve.

Another part of your action plan, as Tony Robbins teaches, is "trade your expectations for appreciation and your whole world will change in an instant." You must cultivate more gratitude. If you are stuck find the goodness; find the gratitude that you have in these goals that you've set. It might be being grateful that you were born in a country that allows you to have goals. Imagine if you didn't have access to education or clean water or medical care. We are an entitled bunch and sometimes we get overwhelmed by the simplicity of how we can live an extraordinary life and wind up in that self-loathing space.

The last thing you see on the Vision/Purpose Statement form is a section for questions. These should be the same three questions that you ask yourself every day to know that you are on track. Mine are: Did I make an impact in somebody's life today? Did I bring joy to myself and others? Did I help somebody reduce suffering? I've had these same questions for the last five years.

I can easily feel successful by keeping it this simple. In the beginning though, when I was building my business I asked questions like: "Did I meet with three potential clients today?" "Did I meet with two REALTORS® today?" "Did I make it a point to share gratitude with others today?"

Often we complicate things too much. We go to bed disappointed because we've made our vision or purpose too tied to productivity, financials, or other things instead of just how we make people feel. When looking at your vision, keep in mind that people will remember you for how you made them feel, not what you actually did.

> *"What you get by achieving your goals*
> *is not as important as what you*
> *become by achieving your goals."*
>
> — Zig Zigler —

Business Plan

"Planning is bringing the future into the present so you can do something about it now."

— Alan Lakein —

I talked about your goals needing to be action-oriented and putting together an action plan. For those goals that are specific to your business your action plan will more commonly be known as your business plan. Ironically most sources I've read say that only about 5% of loan officers have a business plan. Instead what they have is an idea of what they want to do and what they want to produce or make monthly. Often these "ideas" are not based on market data coming out of the Mortgage Bankers' Association nor have anything to do with their own past success or conversion rates. So even though they have business and financial goals they've never put the steps in place to bring them to fruition.

There are several reasons why you need a written business plan just like you need a written vision and goals. First, it allows you to share your strategy, priorities, and specific action steps with your spouse, significant other, management team, and partners. I mentioned earlier to assess who you might need to support you in evaluating the validity of your goals. The same is true here. You want others to support your business plan so you need to share it with them so they can align their actions with yours or at least understand when you might have to put in that 60 hour week.

Second, it helps you to deal with displacement. That means whatever you do is something else you don't do. I spoke a lot about making conscious decisions. This is one of them. When you consciously decide to spend your time or other resources doing a particularly thing to move your business plan forward, you've also consciously decided not to do something else. Being aware that you've already made these decisions keeps you from falling into distraction traps.

Third, it is the primary vehicle by which you grow your business and in turn develop new business alliances and referral partners. Here is where the metrics start to payoff. The primary purpose of putting this together is so you have the data for what you should be doing every day and understand the levers that control the desired output you want.

A solid business plan includes the following: your business vision, your production and activity goals, your levers (where you get business from and how you plan on increasing them), a non-negotiable activity plan, and a marketing plan. I also include my I AM statements for business as a reminder to focus on mindset as well.

I always begin a business plan by re-writing my vision and business goals. I then look at what output measurements are needed that will ensure I meet my goals based on the past year. In our business there are several goals you can use but one of the most effective is to look at activity metrics and not just productivity in terms of loans closed. For example:

- How many face to face meetings do I need to have with Real Estate Agents?

- How many database calls do I need to make weekly?

- How many referrals do I need to receive weekly?

- How many customers do I need to run credit on?

- How many pre-approvals do I need to issue?

- How many loans do I need to pipe or submit to underwriting?

- What percentage of purchase business versus refinance business do I need to be at?

If you look at these metrics from prior years then you'll be able to come up with annualized numbers. You may not have these formulated yet so you will need to go back to every loan you closed and find the source. Come up with the percentage of business you got from each place. You should increase your activity levels and production goals to develop a sustainable business.

You also need to work on increasing your conversion. This will require that you look back to the previous year and see what percentage of pre-approvals closed and what pull-through you had. You can do this with database calls and REALTOR® meetings too. Figuring out how many calls you need to make to book a deal or meeting will help you set new goals. For example, if last year you converted pre-approvals at 25%, a great new goal would be to increase it to 40%. Just doing this will increase the number of loans you fund.

Doing what you've done in the past will only sustain you for as long as the market remains stable. And in this business that's highly unlikely. Besides, producing the exact same results time and again breeds boredom, which leads to more visits by the Instant Gratification Monkey, and before you know it, the business is in a slump.

I would not make the mistake like many loan officers of only having income and volume goals. There are two things that may happen if you do. First, you may not feel successful if you miss the mark, but if you exceed your goals you may lose momentum. If you keep them to things in your control, like activities, then you feel more power and success. There are too many instances where you are almost there but then something crazy happens and you miss your numbers by one loan. Instead of feeling bad, you can remind yourself you did everything in your power and that one loan shouldn't affect your state long-term.

Your business plan should have all your current sources of business and what goals you have to increase them. I call these your Lead Funnels. One of the easiest ways to build this is to look at what you've done in the past year and where the business came from. What percentage was from repeat business, database mining, REALTOR® referrals, or other referral partners? In Level 3 we will go through the potential sources that can increase business.

I have found that most of us get the majority of business from just three funnels. If you are purchase focused those three would usually be your database, database referrals, and REALTORS®. For others it may include builders or a real estate company you are assigned to. If you haven't been purchased focused your funnels may have been lead generation or affinity relationships. It doesn't matter what you determine are your top three because you can always have more funnels from which you get business.

I would suggest that you only spend time and money on three though or you will spread yourself too thin and not master any funnel. I watch loan officers try and chase opportunities from lead sources that have never been proven in this industry to be sustainable. You will eventually learn the hard way if you don't stay focused on what is proven to create a consistent supply of business.

The most important funnel of your business should be your database. These are the customers that have closed a loan with you and know what level of service you provide. They will have future needs to either refinance or purchase. Knowing they will come back to you for any financial or real estate questions will give you more opportunity to help them again.

There are so many things you can do to ensure that they use you in the future. You must consider the data on how long they will stay in their home and where rates are to understand how much business you will get from your database. You should be tracking rates and equity positions so that you can quickly tell people within your database when they might have an opportunity to take advantage of the market. Interest rate fluctuations or program changes will help your business if you are database focused. You will be able to help those people reduce their interest or reduce/improve their mortgage insurance rate if you stay on top of them.

Most loan officers don't do a great job of staying in contact when they believe the customer is in a good position. Remember that not only are you trying to be proactive about helping them with their loan needs but also everyone they know. You won't be likely to do this if you don't invest time in building a relationship with them.

Database referrals are the next funnel. I recommend that you have a "Referral Efficiency" target. This gives you something super clear to shoot for instead of just saying I work by referral. Since your database knows how you operate they will feel more confident referring friends, family and co-workers to you.

A referral efficiency target answers the question that so many loan officers don't know to ask: "How many referrals per year do you get from every customer you close a loan for?" I believe you should get at least two over a twelve month period from the date of the closing. This is not an industry standard metric, it's one that I've devised within this coaching system. You will want to review your business and calculate what yours has been historically.

Here's why it works: let's say I close five loans per month or 60 loans per year. I know if I hit my target of two referrals then I'm going to have at least 120 referrals over the course of the next twelve months. Then I can track conversion on those and have some clarity on what business I will have. That gives me the predictability I need to keep my business sustainable. You can also increase this metric as you get better at mining for referrals. This is the way you get your business to multiply instead of just adding one loan after another.

To do this consistently you need to create a blueprint, a process that says the first time you speak to a customer you tell them, "My goal is to do a phenomenal job with your loan. You will know the status every step of the way and I will be your advocate in getting your deal done. In return, I would appreciate over the course of the next year that you send at least two referrals my way." We will go over this more in Database

Management as it requires a recipe that will ensure you hit your Referral Efficiency target.

The next largest source of business if you are purchase focused should be REALTORS®. They still control anywhere between 50–70% of where buyers choose to do their loan. Although we should be working harder as an industry to find buyers before they get to a REALTOR®, we have to deal with the reality of our current market. They are powerful in directing buyers to a lender. That means you also want to have a "REALTOR® Efficiency" target.

Determining this requires assessing exactly how many referrals you get each month from an agent. For a simple example let's say you have five agents who refer business to you. Two of them send you two referrals per month so you rate them a 2. One sends you three per month so they're a 3. The last two send you six in a year so they're each a half. If you add those up you would be able to say with some predictability that you can expect eight loans to be referred to you each month and that your average is a 1.6 for your REALTOR® Efficiency.

The way I look at it, a REALTOR® needs to be referring at least one referral to you a month or twelve a year to be considered a true referral source. The ideal goal though is to find REALTORS® that refer at least two buyers to you monthly. The internet has changed the distribution of business between selling agents. They are spread out among many more REALTORS® so you need a lot more than you did in the past. If you want to double your production you could say, well I convert 50% of these referrals so I can either double my agent count or I can help the agents I already work with to double their business.

Knowing your REALTOR® Efficiency Ratio will give you clarity about what business you can expect right now and exactly how many more REALTORS® you need to add. The lower the referral efficiency doesn't necessarily mean the lower the maintenance of that REALTOR®. Some who refer you very little business will demand a lot of you. Understanding this metric can guide you to let go of some agents that are just a waste of time, energy, and money.

Another aspect of your REALTOR® plan should include a Listing Agent Efficiency target. This is the percentage of listing agents you convert into long-term referral sources. You have a higher likelihood of adding, these than REALTORS® you have never done business with IF you do a great job communicating and setting expectations. A good target would be to convert 50% to Referring REALTORS®. You will want to look back at your closed purchase transactions and see what you have done historically. Just adding focus on this will help you add more REALTORS® without having to work as hard as you would cold calling.

Other funnels of business may include financial planners, builders, affinity relationships, networking groups, business owners, insurance agents, escrow officers, lead gen, and many others. The important thing to assess in your business plan is how many of these relationships you have now and if you have a desire to increase them. You will also want to quantify the number of referrals you get on average over 12 months.

You will never want to remove a funnel of business unless it is causing you stress and problems. You can see value in all the funnels but again just focus on putting time and energy into three so that you can master them. Eventually you may become so good at one that you can add another. Or you could hire someone to focus specifically on that other area.

Marketing Strategy

> *"Money coming in means I've made the right marketing decisions."*
>
> — Adam Osborne —

Your marketing strategy should include ways that you will increase and retain business. It includes all the funnels that are already proven to bring you referrals and funded loans but may also include new ways that will expand opportunities for you. In addition it includes all the ways you will promote your business and brand.

Depending on your time and resources you may want to consider the following tactics to include in your strategy:

1. Database and Database Referral Plan: this would include how you plan on staying in contact with

your past clients and asking them for more referrals. I've included more information on this topic under the section on business systems since Database Management is a key area in building a sustainable business.

2. Hosting lunch and learns. This was by far the hallmark of my business. Through these I became a business coach and a strategist for my referral sources and REALTORS®. They received information from me that fueled their own success and helped them build additional business. It was the best use of my time as I didn't have to meet agents one by one but could gather them all into a room. This also allowed them to see me as an influencer in the marketplace; someone who could impart wisdom that might turn into business or happiness for them.

   I could also invite listing agents which got me face to face with them during the transaction. If I needed more REALTORS® for referring business to me I would encourage my existing REALTORS® or Title Partners to bring guests with them. When you exceed 20 Referring REALTORS®, hosting a lunch and learn or event is the only way to see them all on a monthly basis.

3. Offering a co-branded marketing campaign to individual real estate agents or real estate companies. A co-branded campaign shows that you are as interested in helping them grow their business as you are in having them help you grow yours.

Low inventory markets add additional pressure to convert pre-approved buyers. Helping your REALTORS® find new listings for these buyers will help fuel business for both of you. Many of your REALTORS® are not good at database management or measuring their conversion rates so helping them become more productive and business-minded will increase your business.

4. Give REALTORS® a solution for turn-downs or for when problems arise by becoming their backup lender. Many loan officers use this to open doors with a REALTOR® that has had a long-term lender relationship with someone else. When an agent tells you they already have a lender you respond with something like: "I understand that you have a preferred lender, but if there's ever a situation when the customer is turned down or is unhappy with the lender, I would love to be that backup person for you."

    Sometimes a deal is about packaging and you can learn a lot from a turn-down to help obtain an approval from a different lender. Being a backup is not a bad place to be because you never know what will happen. I had over 100 REALTORS® in the Sacramento area when I retired from originating. All of those lenders in backup quickly became their preferred lenders because they were patient and willing to be in that position. With the average

age of loan officers reaching 52 we will continue to see more people retire.

5. Refine your value proposition within your market area. Communicate differently about why someone should do business with you and add new creative ways to help them. For example, at my company we have an upfront pre-approval through underwriting which allows the buyer to make a non-contingent offer. REALTORS® can market this to potential listings as a way to close quickly. Look at your existing operations platform and see what you do that provides benefit: maybe it's your programs, maybe it's your process, or maybe it's interest rates.

6. Deliver marketing materials in person to your referral sources monthly. Too many loan officers get stuck at their desk and don't ritualize seeing their REALTORS® face-to-face. Remember the old adage, out of sight, out of mind.

    I love the pop-by idea that Brian Buffini introduced me to in 1998. Get creative with your slogans and always bring "extras" for REALTORS® that you might meet within their office. Some of my all-time favorites were cell phone chargers that had a "Charge your business up with the right partner" slogan attached to them.

7. Set your prospects up in a drip campaign that is unique and includes multiple forms of communication.

You want to do this in order to remain top of mind knowing that you are dealing with a very diverse market. Too often people get prospects but they don't convert them because they don't have a formula for staying in contact. Find a customer relationship management system (CRM) that is familiar with mortgage and has marketing messages already done for a turn-key solution. We will cover this more within business systems.

8. Determine your twelve month marketing campaign at the beginning of the year. What is your quarterly database call going to be around? What mailing pieces are you going to send to you customers, prospects, REALTORS®, or other referral partners? Pre-deciding on this plan allows you to execute on it regardless of what else is going on in your business. You don't need to spend energy trying to figure it out. You can find a resource to build this on my website.

9. Increase buyer prospects. You should constantly be identifying ways that you can increase the number of potential buyers who land on your doorstep. You may go to open houses, you may do a lead campaign, or you may work social media. Whatever it is, keep part of your focus on increasing potential buyers. This can help you build more REALTOR® relationships as well if you have an opportunity to refer them.

10. Increase your listing agent conversion. This involves taking the business you already have and soliciting a deeper relationship with the listing agent who is not already a part of your referral network. Capitalize on the fact that these listing agents are already doing business and have experience with you. Come up with a marketing plan that might include mailing an introduction card, stopping by their office, and then trying to meet them after you successfully close the deal on time.

Remember the goal is to try to convert 50% of those listing agents into long-term referral partners. To put it into quantifiable terms, that means if you are doing four purchases a month now, you should be actively adding two new REALTORS® every single month to your referral database without ever having to cold call agents. Don't have any regrets about not having done this before. It's never too late to go back and pull the names of the agents you had smooth transactions with the year before. Simply apologize for not having contacted them sooner.

Your marketing strategy will be customized to your lead funnels and your strengths. There is no right or wrong. It can be one page or ten pages. It may or may not include diverse segments or demographics. It will depend on whether you want to increase business in those areas. If you prefer the phone, make more calls; if you love meeting people face-to-face schedule more presentations and meetings. You get to decide what works best for your unique personality and style. The important thing to remember is to have a marketing strategy that you have committed to and have built into your schedule and plan.

Non-Negotiable Activity Plan

The next part of your business plan must include a non-negotiable activity plan that you can commit to. This is where you add all the tasks from your marketing plan in an executable format. No matter what, you're going to execute this winning formula every single week of the year that you work. You create a foundation that regardless of how busy you get, no matter how frustrated, you know that these activities are your blueprints for success and sustainability. Many of those non-negotiables will include activities around your marketing strategy. You can have a weekly plan or break it out by the day.

The most important thing to recognize is that these activities need to be done regardless of how many loans you take or loan level problems you face. If you have never read the **Compound Effect** by Darrin Hardy you should. He has taught me it is the things you do every day that add up to long-term success. Here's an example of a non-negotiable plan.

Monday:

- Email/text/call to agents—buyer updates/loan comparisons from weekend and see if they have open house prospects

- 5 calls to Prospect or Database
- Facebook / LinkedIn Post about weekend open houses or market updates
- 5 REALTOR® Calls

Tuesday:

- 5 calls to database
- Process Prospects for the following week: Mail thank you notes, schedule follow-up, add to social media and your CRM.
- Follow up on Refinance Prospects
- 1 REALTOR® Meeting
- 5 REALTOR® Calls

Wednesday:

- Add contacts to database—buyer / new contacts you have just met
- 5 calls to database
- 1 REALTOR® Meeting
- 1 Sphere of Influence Meeting
- Review pre-approved database for credit expiration dates, updated docs and make calls to anyone who needs updated info
- Call REALTORS® that have new listings to target open houses

Thursday:

- 5 calls to database
- 1 REALTOR® meeting

Friday:

- Facebook / LinkedIn: update weekend availability
- 5 calls to database
- Call pre-approved and prospective buyers
- Call REALTORS® with pre-approved buyer updates (rates, programs, etc.)
- Email/Text/Call REALTORS® with weekend availability

Regardless of the metrics and activities you put into your plan, it won't do you any good unless you know the results. Once a week it's important to look at how you performed in each of the activities you set and critical that you evaluate the results from those activities. Give yourself a report card. It's really the only way to see if your plan is working. If it isn't you'll be able to make adjustments each week to do more of the things that create the results you want. You won't be left at the end of the year wondering why you didn't meet your goals. My weekly tracker looks like this but you will want to customize it based on what you decide you want to do:

Weekly Activity Update

- Process Prospect Opportunities: Add to Refinance Prospect Drip or Pre-Approved Buyer Drip in CRM, connect on LinkedIn and Facebook and schedule follow-up call

- Added new REALTORS® or Referral sources into CRM

- Made _____ outbound calls to my database or sphere

- Made _____ outbound calls to my REALTOR® database

- Made outbound calls to pre-approved buyers

- Attended _____ open houses

    Names:

    _____

    _____

    _____

    _____

    _____

- Had _____ meetings with REALTORS®

    Names:

    _____

    _____

    _____

    _____

    _____

- Had _____ meetings with other Referral Sources

    Names:

    _____

    _____

    _____

    _____

    _____

Other Activities:

❏ _____

❏ _____

❏ _____

❏ _____

Results

___ Credit Pulls

___ Pre-Approvals

___ Piped Loans

___ Funded Loans

___ REALTOR® Relationship Confirmed

___ REALTOR® Referrals

___ Database Opportunities

___ Database Referrals

Although activities are important to measure you also need to see what results you are getting so you can make adjustments quickly.

I AM Statements

As you build your business plan you want to take another look at the I AM statements you developed in Level 1 so that you will become the person that can execute on all of this. It will also help you devise the activities that you put into your plan. For instance, if you're someone that had a scarcity mindset in the past, you might have built an I AM list that includes things like I AM prospering, I AM confident, I AM trusting, I AM patient, to go along with an abundance mindset. Adding new activities that will stretch you or are outside of your comfort zone will help reinforce this list.

Or you might be someone that struggles with time management who has I AM statements like, I AM organized, I AM prioritizing my business daily, I AM not distracted easily. You would then include new time management strategies like a weekly planner in your Business Plan. Reminding yourself of the new you and creating your activities based on what this person can do, not what the old person would do, is the key to building a new mindset.

There is a copy of a sample business plan that you can use on my website. Just remember it really doesn't matter if you do it on a napkin or in some elaborate format, what matters is that you are committed to doing whatever it takes to reach your goals. Once you have a solid business plan created, you need to think about what systems you need to handle it all. Chances are you don't have a documented process now to ensure that you are consistent and communicate as effectively as possible.

Following the business systems proposed in the next section will allow you to continuously improve on your conversion rates, deepen relationships within your database, and enhance your Referral Efficiency, and REALTOR® Efficiency targets.

But before I leave these sections on business plans and marketing strategies, it is important to note that none of this will be achievable if you don't have a budget. Sure there are items that only cost time, but there are others like co-branded marketing and lunch and learns that require real dollars. We all know you need to spend money to make money, right? Just don't set your business plans and marketing strategies up to fail simply because you didn't think about the fact that you can't currently afford what you want to do. Set a realistic budget and then get creative stretching those dollars for the greatest impact. If your company doesn't pay your marketing expenses, a good target is 10% of your annual income. If you haven't done this in the past, I can guarantee you have missed out on closing more loans.

Business Systems

> *"I must create a system or be*
> *enslaved by another man's . . ."*
> — William Blake —

For your business to be successful you need to have a processing flow that is documented from start to finish. You can create massive opportunity but if you don't have a solid plan to handle it all, you will not convert well or create the experience needed to ensure your clients come back and refer you to other people.

Your business system is made up of three parts: opportunity—which is how you prospect and nurture leads, pipeline management—which is how you handle deals in progress, and database management—which is how you keep in contact with your past clients and mine for referrals from them. Within each of these sections you have blueprints or recipes. These are the written step-by-step formulas that you use to accomplish the things you do. Most companies can't hand you these business systems. They can tell you to do this or that but it's rare to find a company or mentor that will give you written instructions on the best way to prospect, or work your database, or manage your pipeline.

It still amazes me that our industry lacks this level of professionalism and the technology required to succeed. This is an important commitment because most of us believe that with today's technology improvements, you will no longer be able to close 2–3 loans a month and make the income you currently do. You will need to close more loans and have more referral sources because margins are being compressed and the cost to produce a loan is too high. Compensation is the likely area companies will reduce as they provide an easier way to get loans closed.

If you aren't by nature a person who has a lot of discipline and structure in your business, writing out these blueprints or recipes—how do I handle leads referred, how and when do I communicate during the process, and how do I stay in touch with my database after closing—will give you a consistent method of performing these tasks. And because you're doing the same task the same way every time, if it's not working you know that it's your blueprint, not some random variable. The beauty of a blueprint is that you can modify or change it.

Opportunity

An important aspect of prospecting is creating an experience and process flow for how you handle any lead or referral. Whether on the phone or in person you should decide ahead of time what discussion flow and tools you're going to use. You will also share this with anyone that refers business to you so they know what to expect as well.

You should perform the initial meeting as if it were a presentation. First you tell the prospect what you're going to talk about, then you talk about it, and last you recap what you talked about. You should include dos, don'ts, and potential deal killers that you have encountered in the past. If you do this, you're setting yourself apart from the competition.

When I shared my presentation materials I would tell clients we are a yellow post-it note industry and it is rare they will receive anything in writing. If they ended up meeting with a competitor, they were already comparing how we handled the initial meeting. Another option is to also present them with written payment quotes from a company like Mortgage Coach or Cloud Virga.

Your blueprint or recipe should ensure that every time you are presented with a deal you go through the same ritual. You utilize an intake form. You send a thank you card to the customer and the referral source. You put them in your prospecting campaign within your CRM that includes calls and emails, you add them to social media, etc. You also track the source of the referral or lead so you can better measure your lead funnels and conversion rates. All of this is decided and documented upfront because you know exactly what the blueprint calls for.

This business system is all about how you handle new leads. It is a blueprint or recipe that contains everything from what to do when you receive a lead, to pre-approving the customer, to what you do when they write an offer. As you know, meetings often lead you down crazy paths and you cannot afford to miss covering something with the client that is important. Having folders prepared upfront that include marketing pieces and info on what you need to cover will keep you on track. Think of this as part of your brand. You create replicable buyers that all have the same knowledge and experience.

Think of this aspect of your business as manufacturing qualified and educated customers. Your pre-approval letters will have more power in your market if everyone knows the process you took the buyer through.

You will also be able to create a rating system that includes the difficulty of the transaction and how long you project it will take them to move to a real deal. Deciding upfront what percentage of difficult deals you are willing to take on will help you manage your business better. Taking on more than 10% rush deals or 10% credit challenged borrowers may cause more stress than you can handle so be selective about who you move from a prospect to a real deal.

Pipeline Management

You need to create a process flow and communication system that you can use once a deal enters pipeline. You know exactly what it is you are supposed to be doing every step of the way. You know what your role and responsibilities are as well as the roles and responsibilities of others. You know the deadlines you need to stick with based on contingency removal dates and close of escrow dates. You also have a timeline for closing refinances. In my company we have a process flow and email template system built with detailed steps for every single milestone that happens in the process:

1. Welcome to buyer.
2. Welcome call and email to selling and listing agents.
3. Appraisal received.
4. Approval received.
5. Conditions sent or clear to close submission.
6. CD issued and docs ordered
7. Docs in title and signing arranged
8. Loan funded

Included in our templates are communications designed to let the customer know what they should expect and gives them consistent updates along the way. They set deadlines for clients and REALTORS® for receiving documents that will keep them on track. They also ask for referrals and feedback. We waste too much time writing the same emails and using more energy that we need to.

If your company doesn't provide these types of email templates for your purchase timeline then it's your responsibility to create them. Most email servers will allow you to save them so they are easily accessible to you, your team, and operations staff.

The process flow also contains reminders for what you should be doing through the entire process. Things like discussing the property condition or value at the welcome call to the REALTORS® and talking about funds to close or conditions sent with the buyer to minimize funding issues will help identify concerns earlier. We all need to be kept on track with what we need to do so that we don't end up with deal killer situations.

Having a purchase timeline that works backwards and is on your calendar will ensure that if you are behind you can notify parties immediately. Don't be one of those loan officers who waits until they are behind to request a rush and then places the burden for their lack of management on the operations team. Your business will run so much smoother when you have a pipeline system in place.

Managing your pipeline with consistency is the key to ensuring your database will come back to you for future loan needs and refer clients to you. It will also differentiate you with REALTORS® because their biggest complaint is that they have to ask for updates from their loan officers. You are winning if they never ask for updates and have trust that you manage your pipeline the same with every referral they send to you. Your goal should be to address every potential pitfall throughout the process.

Although your team also has responsibilities for execut-ing the process, ultimately the customer experience falls on your shoulders. You need a checks and balances system so if something falls through the cracks or a service level agreement is missed you can communicate quickly.

The most important aspect of the deal is at funding so attend your signings and be sure that the escrow companies or attorneys know exactly what to expect next. If your borrower's funds to close or fees differ you must ensure that they understand exactly what happened or you could lose them as a long-term customer and referral source. Verifying funds to close or funds received was one aspect of my business I rarely trusted anyone on my team to handle. I also always knew when my clients signed and when we expected funding because of how important this was.

Database Management

If you have done a good job managing opportunity and your database, you should have clients that come back to you for their loan needs and refer other opportunities to you. How you manage your database long-term will determine how successful you are in creating a sustainable business. You should be able to get 50% or more of your business from your database and their referrals.

Most loan officers have the best of intentions in managing their database but if you don't have a system set up it will be difficult to do especially when you get busy. Building a system that you commit to upfront will ensure that in any market you follow through on obtaining as much business as possible. Our industry funding average of just over two loans per originator proves this is an area everyone can get better at. Without a good database management system this would be impossible.

An effective and efficient way to manage your database is to choose the right Customer Relationship Manager (CRM) that does the follow-up and tracking for you. It takes into consideration your marketing plan and holds you accountable. Having a CRM that sends emails, tracks interest rates, and includes direct mail will make it easier to stay in touch. It should also tell you when clients have birthdays and loan anniversaries so you have an opportunity to call them. I would highly recommend using Top of Mind as they have hit on all the important points required to successfully manage your database.

Here is the blueprint or recipe that I recommend once you close a loan. It should gain you the Referral Efficiency target of two referrals for every closed loan you have.

After Funding:

Make the funding call yourself and remind them of your goal to receive 2 referrals that year from them.

Send a thank you to their home and work that includes 5 business cards.

Send an email to obtain online testimonials on publicly searched websites like Zillow or Yelp. Follow up three times to ensure this was completed.

Add them to your CRM if you don't have a company that does this for you.

Send a closing gift to the customer.

Send thank you notes or pop-by to see the REALTORS®.

Add all parties to social media.

Schedule monthly or quarterly calls with your CRM or put them on your calendar.

Add REALTORS® to your REALTOR® Prospect List

At Day 45:
Review the client's loan application and all other loans they have so you can start tracking any opportunities they have to refinance. A good CRM may have the capability to add multiple loans so you can track future interest rate benefits.

Call the client and ensure they received their monthly statement information and see if they have any referrals for you. Ask if they have any long-term life changes that you can add to your calendar. Remind them again your goal is to have them send at least two referrals to you.

Long-Term Maintenance:
Email or mail to them monthly

Call quarterly

Post on social media weekly

Setting up reasons and scripts within your marketing plan will keep you committed to making calls. A lot of people don't call because they don't know what to say. Having a reason to call scripted upfront will ensure you actually make your calls. You need to build long-term relationships with your database so they trust you to send information to their family, friends or co-workers. Every call is also an opportunity to remind them you love referrals and update any anticipated life changes.

The reason it is important to post on social media is to remain top of mind. The filtering system within their brains may forget to refer you if they aren't in contact with you. You can manage most social media accounts to only allow certain content to be seen by business contacts, or you can maintain a separate business page if that makes you more comfortable. You can also look at hiring someone to do this for you. Sharing testimonials online from your database will also help reinforce referrals.

Managing your database contact consistently will enable you to receive and track referrals and business better. If you have 500 closed clients now and you do two loans per month from past clients and close one referral a month, you will know when you get to 1000 you will likely have doubled your business. The actual metrics depend on your referral efficiency rate and conversion rates so make sure you track them. You never want to get so purchase-focused that you miss out on this business because you don't have a proven business system that takes care of it for you.

It will bring certainty and clarity to what you are doing. Once you reach a certain point, you may be able to hire someone full-time to manage your database and calls. Just assess what you like to do and what you don't so you can easily handoff things long-term that you know bring business.

I helped over 2500 clients with their loan needs in my career and was comfortable that no matter what I had 20 loans that I was certain to close just from my database and their referrals. I did reach the point that I could put my feet up and only focus on this one funnel if I wanted to. Committing to building this system before you reach that level will help you ensure that when you get busy you won't ever stop focusing on it.

Level 2 has helped you build your vision, goals, business plan and created systems that will ensure you communicate consistently. It is now time to start executing on your plan in Level 3.

LEVEL 3
EXECUTING

———

"Plans are only good intentions unless they degenerate into hard work."
— Peter Drucker —

In Level 1 we laid the footers to support our foundation by working on our mindset and who we are being. Then in Level 2 we did the framing, giving our vision, goals, and business plan the structure our business needs to flourish. Now in Level 3 we get to implement what we have designed. We get to do all the things that will make our foundation sustainable, able to weather any storm. We get to execute. You will not have sustainable success unless hard work and executing are a top priority.

If you've dreamt big enough, your vision, your goals, your business and marketing plans are going to catapult you out of your comfort zone. Even with your activity planner broken down into small, manageable pieces, you may still feel a bit overwhelmed on that first day of action. Level 3 is all about the "how tos" of executing your plan. We're going to talk about idea and opportunity creation, nurturing and creating new referral sources, branding, daily disciplines and accountability, assessing our daily state to prevent burn out or ruts, and building teams. I'm going to give you examples of how you can execute in each of these categories. You can select what works for you, or better yet, use these as a springboard for your own creativity.

The importance of execution cannot be overstated. I've said this before and I'll say it again—you can't simply "think" your way into success. I wish we could. Then we'd all be wildly successful and no one would have any need for this book. If you're not an action-oriented person by nature then this could be a bit scary. But trust me once you begin with the small steps, the larger ones get easier.

Execution is about discipline. It's about commitment. Execution is not giving up the first time something doesn't work right but keeping at it, constantly tweaking until it does. Execution is about sticking to your activity plan even when you don't feel like doing it.

You can never escape hard work so be sure that if your work ethic isn't high you make a new commitment to yourself and your business. If you are coming out of a season of burn-out where everything is frustrating you, you will need to do some deeper mindset work before you start executing. If you don't love the business but love the money, then this will be more difficult for you but it is possible to still be super successful. I know a ton of top producers that don't love the business and approach it like a job rather than a passion.

Idea and Opportunity Creation

"Opportunity dances with those already on the dance floor."

— H. Jackson Brown, Jr. —

When I talk about opportunity in the mortgage business I'm really talking about lead generation. A lead is the name and contact information for someone who is potentially a future client. It should be your primary focus as you learned in the core beliefs you should maintain. All referrals can be thought of as leads, but not all leads are referrals. A lead can come from a service like Zillow, or it could be from a cold call list you bought from a marketing firm.

Leads may also be qualified or unqualified. An unqualified lead may be unsure of what you offer. They may not know what they need or your programs may be out of their budget. While it's possible to convert unqualified leads, the conversion rate is low. People who are shopping for homes fall into this category because they haven't asked for a loan or pre-approval.

Qualified leads on the other hand know exactly what they are looking for. They have a general idea of the solution they need and are most likely aware of your company. Qualified leads often come from your referral sources or other sources where someone specifically is looking for a loan. They are far easier to convert.

Garnering the right leads for your business requires knowing what your ideal customer looks like. You need to create a vision of who that client is—age, income level, business owner or employee, education, etc. Once you know their demographics and attributes you can share the vision of your ideal client with your referral sources so they can send more of those types your way.

The easiest way to determine your ideal client is to go back twelve months and spend time thinking about all the transactions that you've done. Which ones had clients that you really valued working with? What was it about them you enjoyed? Were they better educated? Did they understand lending and finance concepts easier? Were they willing to trust your advice? Were they all first-time homebuyers or retirees looking to downsize?

The next thing you want to do is determine your "why." Why is it important to you to help these families? What can you do better than anyone else to service them?

Your first inclination will probably be that you want to make money. But that's rarely the real reason why you do what you do. Dig deeper. Clients instinctively know when you are truly interested in being of service to them rather than lining your pockets. Doing this will help you stay focused on the vision of your perfect client and bring you more joy in working with them.

You get to choose where you get your business so let's explore the top opportunity sources and creative ways to get more business from them.

Database and Referrals

*"The quality of your life is determined
by the quality of your relationships.
The quality of your business is no different."*

— Harvey Mackay —

The individuals within your database are prime candidates for finding leads. Most of them know you and have experience working with you. In your activity planner and Database System, you should have committed to making this a priority.

When I do a working by referral presentation I often jokingly remark that loan officers think working by referral is accepting them when someone sends them to them. Unfortunately, it isn't a joke for many of them. They haven't mastered the art of cultivating referrals. They are the ones who end up with reactive referral sources. A reactive source is one who when specifically asked will say, sure you should go to this loan officer.

What you want to create are pro-active referral sources. They are the ones who overhear somebody talking about needing a mortgage or buying a new home and interject with your information without being asked. The way to do this is by setting the scene upfront.

As you execute on making calls to your database, you will want to assess the current market to see if they can benefit from rate or program changes, and if you have gotten any referrals from that person. If you remember, your goal is to obtain two referrals per year. You will want to remind people of that every time you speak to someone and see if they have any upcoming life changes.

Life changes such as divorce, death, graduations, retirement, or job changes should monitored. You can do this by following your clients on social media and asking the right questions as you make your calls.

Your database can also connect you to other referral sources. Asking refinance clients to introduce you to their original REALTOR® or other professionals may also open doors for new opportunity. Especially ask refinance clients if they bought within the last two years.

As you make your calls identify any clients that work at companies or businesses that you may want to target. You can increase the number of referrals you receive by sending items to their work. Dropping off sandwich trays or cookies at a larger office will ensure that you have access to more people they know. I found that nurse's stations, Doctor's offices and technology offices were prime places for me to target. If your client works in HR, also ask them about providing homebuyer workshops for their employees.

If your client is in a job where they too are dependent on referrals see if there are ways you can work together. For example, you could collaborate with a financial planner on providing a mortgage update at their next seminar.

Behavioral marketing and digital leads can help you find clients that match the vision of your perfect client. However, they are harder to work because they weren't personally referred to you. This is where your online testimonials will help you gain their trust faster. If you have 50 clients on Zillow that praise your service, then a new client will more feel more confident in using you.

Behavioral marketing is a social media strategy that finds clients that are likely to buy or refinance. You will need to hire a firm to help with this unless you enjoy this type of marketing. Leads would include prospects by areas you target like veterans or first time homebuyers.

Digital leads are leads that you can either work on with a real estate agent (co-marketing) or purchase on your own. You can buy digital leads from aggregators like Lending Tree and Zillow. If you have a plan to work them they can be a good place for some loan officers to start. By plan I mean a commitment that no matter what, you're going to call the leads quickly and follow up daily. A good lead to call timeline is less than 5 minutes. 1 minute is ideal but the longer you wait the less likely you will catch them. You will also need a long-term recipe to nurture them. If you don't execute your plan then you're just wasting your money on this opportunity.

When you do co-branded campaigns ensure you have an agreed upon protocol to capture these leads even if the client chooses not to work with the REALTOR®. You can expect a 1–3% conversion rate on these leads so get ready to have a lot of bad phone numbers and clients you never get in touch with.

Whichever lead generation sources you choose, you must schedule your lead generation time. Make it non-negotiable; from this time to this time on Tuesdays and Thursdays, I make lead gen calls no matter what. Put it on your calendar. Make it a priority. You have to connect with prospects quickly or someone else will. Sustainability comes from growth—growth comes from leads.

All of these prospects should be added into your CRM and nurtured. According to the National Association of REALTORS®, the average buyer takes 12 weeks to find a property so it is a long incubation period. There is no data, however, that says how long from when they actually start browsing online. Some of these leads will take longer than others so don't give up too soon.

Nurturing and Creating New REALTOR® and Referral Sources

In your business plan you assessed how many REALTORS® you currently have and what their **REALTOR® Efficiency Rate** is. You also assessed at what rate you convert on these leads. This information tells you if you have enough REALTORS® or need to prospect and target new ones.

You want to retain the ones you have by continuing to pursue them even after they have given business to you. REALTORS® want to know you value them. Schedule regular meetings to review ways you can help support their business. I would suggest you always have a purpose for the meeting. Otherwise you may end up accomplishing nothing. You want to create deep relationships with your Referring REALTORS® but you need to stay focused on your goals. You are always at risk of losing them if you don't stay in contact with them during slow times. Other lenders will be targeting them as well so you must remain in constant pursuit of them.

A great way to stay in front of your Referring REALTORS® is by hosting regular lunch and learns. It may seem intimidating if you haven't hosted one before. Documenting what you need to do will ensure that you have a successful event.

Here is a recipe I have used that worked effectively:

1. Choose and research a subject (see my website for options)

2. Create your guest list

3. Choose a venue (your conference room or a meeting room at a restaurant)

4. Create and send an invitation, evite, or Facebook event

5. Follow up with phone calls for RSVPs

6. Prepare your PowerPoint and handouts

7. Order lunch and drinks

8. Hold the event

9. Follow up after to obtain feedback and ideas for the next one

Usually 25% of the REALTORS® I invited would attend. I recommend the subject be on something that educates and provides ideas for them to create new business. If you aren't comfortable speaking in front of a group, you might want to find a speaker who would do the presentation for you.

It is difficult to retain REALTORS® so always be certain they know what to expect from you and communicate consistently. You should let them know your availability; particularly when you are going to be unavailable. I know REALTORS® that would fire you if one weekend you weren't available to update a pre-approval letter on a hot property they were trying to write an offer on. Updating them weekly on the status of any prospects and clients in your pipeline will minimize the risk of losing them as well.

Chances are you don't currently have enough Referring REALTORS® to reach your goals so you should be actively pursuing new ones. I divide these into Prospective REALTORS® and Targeted REALTORS®. Prospective REALTORS® are either listing agents you had a successful transaction with or agents that you have just met. Targeted ones are those that you haven't done business with or met yet. You have either heard good things about them or were referred to them by someone else. You can also target REALTORS® by their production as well.

Finding new agents is like prospecting for new clients. The first step is to identify your ideal agent. You do this by assessing your current active agents who refer to you. What markets do they specialize in? How many years of experience do they have? You only want to add REALTORS® that meet your criteria. This will ensure you only pursue REALTORS® that you'll enjoy working with.

Here are some ideas for adding both:

Listing Agents are by far the easiest agents to convert. They know what it's like to work with you and have experienced how you communicate. Start off by telling them at the welcome call that your goal is to hit the close of escrow date and if you do you'll be asking them to commit to meeting you for coffee or lunch. Throughout the transaction remind them of their commitment and also continuously ask if you can do anything for them.

REALTORS® who are personally referred to you by a past client, other REALTORS® or Title and Escrow Reps are also easier to book meetings with. I always ask the person who referred me to email an introduction explaining why they are recommending me.

Meeting REALTORS® at open houses can also be a great way to add Prospective REALTORS®. It is easier than cold calling or dropping by their office unannounced. Just be respectful if there are potential buyers or sellers in the home. Have a recipe for follow-up as well so that you set a future meeting with them.

REALTOR® office meetings can help you meet multiple REALTORS® at the same time. Not all offices are closed. You won't know unless you ask the receptionist or manager if you can either stop by or do a presentation. The first presentation I did came from a referral to the owner. Although I probably sucked at the presentation, I found eight new REALTORS® that I eventually ended up working with. This didn't include the listing agents I was able to convert on when I had transactions with them.

Keep your Prospective REALTORS® and Targeted REALTORS® in a nurture campaign similar to the one you have for your Referring REALTORS®. The goal is to move them from one level to the next; ultimately to where you receive referrals from them regularly. Ensure they are added to social media, receive regular calls, and email updates from you.

There are many ways to approach new agents. Coming up with your own unique recipe will make it easier and replicable. I suggest allowing the REALTOR® to talk 90% of the time at your first meeting. Encourage them to share their goals with you and how they typically do business. Ask about past experiences with other lenders and what is important to them.

Knowing this information will allow you to formulate the value proposition you can share with them at your next meeting. As you meet with new REALTORS® calculate your conversion rate. How many REALTORS® do you need to meet with before they become a referral source? Everyone is different because we all have different personalities and offer different products or value propositions.

You don't need scripts but you want to have a strategy and goal for what you want to discuss going in. A good target is to meet with three new REALTORS® weekly even when you have reached your Referring REALTOR® goal. You never know when you will need to replace one.

A lot of loan officers struggle with whether they should target brand new REALTORS®. I wouldn't recommend that you focus completely on it but all top producers were new at one time. I would be highly selective and use your intuition. The worst one to add would be a part-time, new REALTOR®. If you are strategic, you will know that you need to limit the number of new agents you take on at a time.

Always be crystal clear about what you want. Your time is valuable and you aren't trying to build friendships. Too many loan officers focus on being friends first and end up resenting the REALTOR® in the long run. There is nothing wrong with being business-minded and upfront about it. You must be a closer and convert these meetings into long-term referral sources. You need to sit down with each agent and say, "I'm looking to work with agents who want to refer at least two buyer opportunities to me a month." Loan officers have this false belief that REALTORS® only want to work with them if they pay for half their marketing and refer buyers and sellers to them. Yes, an agent is going to have expectations of you, but I'm finding that those things aren't necessarily the value that top producing REALTORS® are looking for.

I've recently started interviewing top producing agents to answer that very question. Here's a sample of my interview with Sonia Immers, top producing REALTOR® at Keller Williams Roseville. She had $26,760,859 in production in 2016. She closed 17 buy-side transactions and referred 13 to her preferred lenders.

Me: What do lenders do to try and get your business that drives you crazy?

Sonia: They stop by my Open Houses and initiate a lengthy conversation with me when I should be conversing with my Open House guests.

Me: If you could isolate three value propositions that your lenders would possess what would they be?

Sonia: I need to be able to count on my lenders; that means all aspects of the Borrower need to be vetted out ahead of time. Any and all potential challenges or hurdles need to be openly discussed and disclosed.

Me: More lenders today are told by REALTORS® that they need to pay for a portion of their marketing OR send them buyer referrals to have a chance to work with them. How do you feel about that?

Sonia: I do not work with my preferred vendors with an expectation of referrals. I choose to work with my preferred vendors because they take the same special care of my clients as I do, always have my client's best interest at heart, and get the job done.

If you'd like to see the results of more of these interviews please email your contact information to my address at the back of this book—place Interviews in the subject line. It may surprise you how many loan officers have false beliefs that stop them from going after more REALTORS®.

It seems easier to work with fewer REALTORS® that refer you more deals per month but the market has changed. There are not many agents that do more than one or two buy-sides a month. You need to research reports in your market to really figure out how many top producers there are and how many transactions they close on average.

While your database and REALTORS® should be your primary referral sources there are other referral sources to consider. As you network and connect with your database, here are a few to consider:

Financial planners—they have influence with their clients. A lot of clients will contact them about paying off debt or moving to a shorter term loan. Many have events that you can collaborate on. I would encourage you to train your financial planners to ask their clients to bring them mortgage statements to their meetings. That way you have an opportunity to evaluate all their clients' loans not just the ones that ask for a referral.

Attorneys of all types—Trust, Divorce, Estate Planning, etc.—get to know the best in each category so you can refer your clients back. There are so many life changes that result in a real estate or mortgage need. Take the time to understand how you can work with them to build more business for both of you.

CPAs—many clients reach out to their CPA about tax implications or benefits before they buy or refinance. Many CPA's send out newsletters that you can advertise in OR you can have you info in their lobby.

Builders—either to be their primary or backup lender. This can be a large funnel of business but you need a full plan to focus on this. You can connect through a successful transaction or target meeting builders through BIA events.

Title and Escrow Reps—they work with some of the top REALTORS® in the market—help them with introductions and obtain REALTORS® you can target. Resale Escrow Officers are very influential and can ensure your name is dropped, especially when deals are falling apart or taking too long.

Other loan officers—while this might seem strange not all loan officers have the ability to offer every type of loan—become their backup. Major banks can pull in and out of certain markets so just remain up-to-date for opportunities with friends you may have at other companies.

Although you should spend the majority of your time focusing on your database, REALTORS® and these other referral sources, if you like networking you will meet people from other industries that can send you business as well. Business owners, hair stylists, teachers, doctors, police officers, etc. are all viable referral sources. It is difficult to spend time targeting these but if you have the opportunity to develop a referral relationship, take it! Add them into nurture campaigns and always remember to reach out and ask for more referrals.

Branding

While you will continue to help all the opportunities that come your way, you can start to build your business and brand around your ideal clients. In fact, your marketing plan should be designed to target as many of them as possible. Every day you are speaking with clients and helping them, you are building your brand.

I could write an entire book around branding but for our purposes think of it as your promise to your customers that you will deliver differentiated benefits if they work with you. These are the things that you do better than your competition or things you do that your competition does not. This is also referred to as your brand's unique value proposition that I spoke about in Level 2. To be of value, you must deliver on your promises consistently at every point of contact with the customer, time after time.

Your brand is not just your logo or your look. It is the way customers or REALTORS® view you. The number of online testimonials you have is the best indication of who you are and what you provide that is outstanding to clients researching you. If your service is a secret between you and your clients, then you aren't building your brand and you are missing opportunities. The reason you include asking for testimonials in your Database System is to ensure you are building your brand every day. You must focus on building the right perception of your brand in the marketplace.

It doesn't take a huge investment in marketing, but it does take some introspection and making a non-negotiable decision about how you want to be perceived. More clients are using the internet to find out about you before they choose to do business with you. Every post you make or testimonial you receive can be accessed by them so be careful what you put out there.

Choose a company like Reach 150 or Social Survey that can help build your brand for you. They will send out the testimonial requests on your behalf and then remarket it to other prospects. They can also share it on social media so your Database and Sphere also see it.

Even if you think you have a negative brand now because you had a few bad transactions or lost a few REALTORS®, you can always change it. We cannot be perfect but we can become committed to getting better and better. Make a decision today that you will remain committed to building a better brand for yourself. Remember every conversation you have is building your brand so keep anything negative or judgmental to yourself. I get a kick out of loan officers and REALTORS® that fire clients on social media or brag about it. This will eventually diminish your brand and cause others to see you poorly.

Your brand must be based on the perception of others not how you see yourself so constantly ask for feedback on what you can do better or improve on. Conduct a semi-annual review with your referral partners and solicit their feedback so you can make quick changes. Sometimes your clients will tell them, rather than you, where you could have done better.

Daily Disciplines and Accountability

In your business plan you created a non-negotiable activity plan that you should be committed to. It includes all the activities you know will ensure you hit your **Referral Efficiency** and **REALTOR® Efficiency** targets. In addition to scheduling time daily to do these things you should also be tracking your results and conversion rates. As markets change, these numbers can change. Asking your manager or a coach to hold you accountable will help ensure you do the things you should be doing even when you don't feel like doing them. I recommend using the Weekly Report so you can make adjustments quickly if you aren't getting the results you need. If you fall short one week just add those activities to the following week. Always do a mid-week check on Wednesday at noon to see where you are. You may need to kick up your activity levels if you have fallen behind.

You also need to make quick adjustments if clients or referral partners cancel. You will want to replace those meetings as soon as possible rather than just telling yourself it is not your fault.

The only person who suffers when you don't do these things is you. The reason it is non-negotiable is that we are all good at making excuses and then complaining that we don't have enough business. You are the one that made your goals and plan so having the discipline to follow through is key. We covered how to do many items on the list earlier in this level so that should make it easier to execute.

Some other items you will want to do daily are to return all calls and emails timely. Even if you don't have the time to spend with them at that moment, calling and setting up another time to talk will help you. Clients can move on quickly if you aren't responsive. Also ensure that your voicemail is never full. If it is full clients and REALTORS® will think you are too busy for their business.

As you get busy, you may want to adopt a more professional approach to taking applications. Offering appointment times rather than taking a half-baked application in your car will guarantee you don't miss anything. Take a full application and don't cut corners by assuming anything. I recommend booking appointments 90 minutes apart so you always have time for fires and call backs in between.

If you aren't executing daily, go back to the sabotage section. It is likely you are the reason you aren't and you will need to work more on your mindset.

Your week should allow time to be creative about your business. This will give you energy and ignite more passion for what you are doing. Leave some time to research new ideas or to meet new people so you can learn how they created success.

Assessing your Daily State

In Level 2 you identified how you can sabotage your own success. Whether you are triggered or encounter file challenges, you have to remain focused on the end result you want to achieve. Assessing your state daily will help you make adjustments quickly. This is a burn out business where we can rapidly get into a funk. Remaining aware of how your state affects your ability to execute will guide you to seek help faster. We all have people in our life that can inspire us or get us out of a funk. Don't delay in seeking out help. You want to have more good days than bad days.

And don't beat yourself up if you do have a bad day. Don't focus on it . . . just move on. Make a commitment to getting back to your plan the next day and give yourself a break. Use the sabotage management plan to ensure that if you do get in a funk you know how to get yourself out. If you get triggered use the four step process and get back to business as soon as you can.

Executing on all you need to do is near impossible to do alone and still continue to grow your business. There is a human capacity to what you can accomplish. We will now dive into team building so you can take part of your plan and start delegating activities.

Team Building

> *"Teamwork makes the dream work."*
>
> — Bang Gae —

There is a limit to what any one loan officer can do alone. I've found when you are purchase focused, the most sustainable way to be, and you start to fund over five loans a month you begin to get overwhelmed. That seems to be the threshold. There are just too many things to do: open houses, putting deals together, working on marketing campaigns, updating your pipeline, hitting your close of escrow dates, trying to manage a database. Something has to give.

Usually it results in a loan officer seesawing between good months and bad months. One month production is up because you've spent your time prospecting. The next month business is down because now you're spending all your time managing the pipeline. Then you shift back to prospecting and the cycle continues. This is why so many loan officers are in scarcity mode much of the time.

To build a sustainable business you must constantly be building your pipeline. The primary function of a loan officer should be creating new business opportunities. When you reach the point where this is no longer possible you must start looking for someone to help you. This usually coincides with good production numbers. Once you reach a certain level you can generally ask for what you need. Most companies are happy to supply assistants if your production continues to go up.

In my experience the first person you should hire is someone who can manage your pipeline. This person will help with your files, with communication, with follow-up and database management so you have time to spend prospecting, meeting with REALTORS®, and focusing on gathering new opportunities.

Before I hired my first assistant, I spent time looking at my job description. I had to create one because my company at the time, like other companies, didn't really tell me what to do. I made a list of all the things I did. At the top of the list I put the things I really enjoyed doing. At the bottom of the list went all the things I hated doing. So when I did hire someone, their job description was already done—they got all the things I hated doing. For most of you that will be the details and follow-up but for others it could be the marketing and prospecting.

As you get beyond the first hire, you'll want to continually refine what you need. You'll be able to pass more responsibility to others. A general rule of thumb is that for every fifteen loans you need one person dedicated to closing that business. Building an effective team allows you to focus on your strengths. For me that meant meeting with customers and REALTORS® face-to-face, hosting monthly REALTOR® lunch and learns, and building a sustainable business.

Building an effective team isn't simply placing a warm body in a seat. Teams are only as good as their leaders. Leaders are only good if they have a clear vision—they know what activities and results need to be measured, they know what needs to be accomplished, and they've provided the team with a roadmap on how to get there. Leaders have built the foundation for their business and they communicate it.

But being a visionary isn't the only requirement of a team leader. You also must be able to manage people. You should set guidelines and measure performance. You must deal with personnel issues. If you're not a leader in this sense of the word, if you identify that your strengths are in opportunity creation and not day-to-day supervision, then hire someone who has the leadership skills to get things done. It should be someone you respect, will be willing to listen to, and has the ability to hold others accountable.

Make sure that you hire the right people. Vet them ahead of time. Ask them what their goals are. When my business was prospering I got people all the time who wanted to work for me. Many of these people just wanted to pick my brain and learn as much as possible from me with the idea that they'd leave after a time to start their own business.

Don't hire anyone you think won't be with you for more than three years. You won't even start to see any benefit from the hire until about six months in after you've spent time training and investing in them. Some of the best lessons I've learned is building teams are:

1. Fire people fast if they aren't a good fit. Negative energy spreads.

2. Have very defined roles with metrics and results attached so you can make good long-term decisions.

3. Believing that a team can take away your stress is nonsense. You should master what you're doing by yourself before you should feel comfortable bringing in new people.

4. It is better to build small and to dial in who you are and what you're doing than to look for somebody to come in and rescue you.

5. You will never escape the responsibility of owning your customer's experience or building your brand. You must own your team's mistakes like you made them yourself. Inspecting their work and continuously training and supporting them are the only ways you will thrive.

6. Continue to build your process and roles and responsibilities. Learn from every file so you reduce any potential mistakes or delays that may occur during the process.

7. If you blame them for issues or treat them poorly or inconsistently, they will leave. For them it is a job and they can find a better one so treat them well.

8. Identify what makes them feel appreciated and praise them often. I love *The 5 Languages of Appreciation in the Workplace*, by Gary Chapman and Paul White as a reference to help ensure they are getting their needs met.

You will not be able to take your business to the next level without letting go of something and building a team. Just be prepared and have a good business plan to share with them so everyone knows what part they play in the team's success.

CONCLUSION

———

"What you get by achieving your goals is not as important as what you become by achieving them."
— Henry David Thoreau —

When you've mastered the concepts of building a foundation for sustainable success, when you've acquired a success mindset, when you've articulated your vision, goals, business plan and marketing plan, when you've put your business systems in place and learned to execute on them, there will come a time . . .

. . . a day where you've created so much opportunity for yourself that you feel you can put your feet up on the desk. You can take your foot off the gas and let certain activities go on auto-pilot. You might even be able to stop doing goals and creating a business plan and still be wildly successful.

Even if you could, should you? There is a challenge to backing off. The moment you stop growing, you start dying. Human nature is to get bored without constant variety and activity. Boredom leads to burn out and burn out leads to a loss of joy. Be aware, if you decide to stop doing some of the steps in building your foundation, you are putting your own joy at risk.

Through Level 1—the footers, you worked on who you are being.

Your mindset and how you manage your emotions are critical to your success. The more you blame and complain the more likely it is that you will remain stuck at the same level year after year. Invest more time in yourself and constantly be growing as a person. Understand what triggers you and make a commitment to reduce your stress levels. If you have amazing success but then die at age 50 from a heart attack it will not have been worth it. Remember sabotage can derail you if you aren't aware and ready for it.

In Level 2—the frame, you created your vision, goals, and plan.

You created a plan that you can follow daily and start compounding the success you have. You decided on your top three lead funnels and have a marketing plan to expand your business.

Finally in Level 3—you implemented the plan, you started executing.

You found you cannot escape hard work and discipline and expect to master this business. You found new ways that you can increase opportunities and receive more referrals. You are taking more time to be creative and find more business. Hopefully you found an accountability partner and are committed to working on your non-negotiable activity plan weekly.

It's been a lot of work. Probably more than you anticipated. You may want to relax and enjoy it for a while. But foundations, no matter how well built, still require maintenance. Otherwise they fall apart. You will need to continuously work on retaining your referral sources and finding new ways to differentiate yourself.

I began this book talking about the inevitability of change in the mortgage industry. You must accept it and become more resilient. If you have been at this for a while you have seen it change so much already and you know that there is more to come. To adapt you need to constantly focus on reinventing yourself and your business. You must keep remodeling so your foundation stays fresh.

There may be a time that you need to close more loans to make the same amount of money. Technology will replace some of what you do so constantly focus on the value of the relationships you build. Companies want to do it faster and cheaper so it is up to us to ensure we do not become obsolete. We have seen the change in other industries but you cannot get a personal touch online so keep focused on that.

You can implement some or all of what I shared in your business. But I believe the most important work you do is on yourself and your mindset. Your ego will lead you to make critical mistakes if you don't. Too many loan officers blame external forces for their drop in production or income. Look carefully at your business and where it comes from and be willing to try new things.

You must take massive action and go against the laziness that exists in our industry. You must find new people to associate with who will support and push you. The saying you are only as successful as your five closest friends is true. You should not limit your own success by failing to plan and surrounding yourself with mediocre people who have no passion or purpose in this business.

If you want to live an extraordinary life where your success and income are limitless this is the industry to be in. There is no cap on your income and it is not difficult to elevate yourself above the competition.

You must stop making excuses and sabotaging yourself by not being disciplined. Even though no one really cares what you do you must find your own "why" that will be the leverage you need to achieve your goals. Your passion may or may not be doing loans but it will set you up to live a prosperous life.

Do not let yourself be an ego-driven jerk, treating others poorly simply because that behavior has become acceptable in our industry. Even if you are a top producer, or may become one, entitlement only leads to long-term suffering. Treating everyone with kindness and gratitude is the only way to be truly successful and happy. You can still hold people accountable but you must remain unaffected emotionally by mistakes or problems.

Most successful businesses have a vision, goals, plans, and rituals that bring them success. Start taking massive action today on building everything you need to thrive. Just start slow and continue to layer in everything you need as you go.

My hope is that by working on these principles together, we will elevate the professionalism of ourselves and the industry as a whole. You can also massively affect your referral partners by sharing the wisdom you learned in this book. Sharing it with others will impact their well-being and level of success.

ABOUT THE AUTHOR

Kelly has more than 20 years of professional growth and success in the mortgage industry. A top producing mortgage originator and loan consultant for the likes of Washington Mutual and Wells Fargo; she now serves as the Executive Vice President of Sales and Business Development for Paramount Partners Group, a residential mortgage lending company.

Before retiring from originating she helped over 2500 families and managed over 100 Referring REALTORS®. She continues to speak and impact loan officers with her Foundation to Sustainable Success system.

Kelly credits part of her success to the strategies she has shared in this book and focusing on referral business. She will also tell you she focuses daily on creating more joy and becoming the best person she can be. The more she has learned on her journey of self-discovery, the more she has seen how the same principles can be used to propel her business forward. This knowledge and wisdom she found in the personal growth world has helped her impact countless loan officers and REALTORS® in building their businesses.

In Foundations to Sustainable Success Kelly enthusiastically shares this knowledge with every loan officer who wishes to grow their business. She is devoted to serving as a leader, as a mentor, and as a resource, offering goal-setting and leadership training that encourages mortgage professionals to excel in their business and better serve the needs of their customers. If you'd like to connect with Kelly you may contact her at: kresendez@foundationtosustainablesuccess.com

Or visit her website at:
www.foundationtosustainablesuccess.com

ACKNOWLEDGMENTS

"Be strong enough to stand alone,
smart enough to know when you need help
and brave enough to ask for it."

— Mark Amend —

There have been so many people in my career that have inspired me and helped me become successful. I am so grateful for Doug Edwards and Wendy Muir for believing in me and giving me the start I needed in the mortgage industry. Alber Saleh, a mega-producer, was my mentor who helped me stay focused on building a sustainable model and provided a mindset I could model. My first REALTOR® and now close friend Gloria Doze, helped me cultivate the vision of my perfect REALTOR® and created countless opportunities for me. Over our 20 years together her love and encouragement has helped me stay focused.

Sarah Shackel has been the rock in my career and has always been there for me personally and professionally. She ran my team and allowed me to enjoy more quality time with my kids and maintain the balance I needed. Many of the systems and ideas in this book were created because of her wisdom and feedback.

I want to thank Hayes Barnard, Matt Dawson, and Jason Walker, the founders of Paramount Equity Mortgage, who gave me the autonomy to build Paramount Partners Group which is based on the principles in this book. I also want to thank my entire team at PPG for the deep friendships we have and for always being willing to implement the FTSS system. You have all helped me try new things and get better clarity about best practices.

There are too many friends to mention that helped support me during my journey but a special mention to Kirsten Vidosh who has always supported my vision and accepted me for who I am.

My family has guided me to become the person capable of living an extraordinary life. Although they are in heaven now, both my mom and grandma pushed me to be hard-working, disciplined, and driven. My dad and my sister Kim continue to be there for me whenever I have needed them. I want to thank Jay Resendez for all his encouragement over the years. And my precious children, Paige and Cole, for loving me unconditionally and being my why for everything I do.

A special thanks to Travis Esway, who has stood by me during this journey. Your support has been priceless to me.

And finally to Caren Cantrell for guiding me during this process and helping me get this vision to the finish line.

77741683R00102

Made in the USA
Middletown, DE
25 June 2018